CHARLOTTE
AND
FEODORA

CHARLOTTE AND FEODORA

A troubled mother-daughter relationship
in Imperial Germany

John Van der Kiste

A & F

First published by Amazon KDP 2012
Revised edition published by A & F 2015

A & F Publications
South Brent, Devon, England, UK

ISBN (13-digit) 978-1514877371
ISBN (10-digit)1514877376

Typeset 11pt Roman
Printed by CreateSpace

Contents

Foreword

This short joint life of Princess Charlotte of Prussia, later Hereditary Princess and then Duchess of Saxe-Meiningen (1860-1919), the eldest daughter of the German Emperor Frederick and granddaughter of Queen Victoria, and her daughter Feodora, later Princess Henry of Reuss (1879-1945), began some years earlier as two articles, one on each, which were first published in 'Royalty Digest' and 'European Royal History Journal' respectively. Details of both appear alongside other sources in the bibliography.

I had long been fascinated by the saga of the Hohenzollern family in the nineteenth and twentieth centuries, and found the none-too-well-documented tale of the fractious relationship between mother and daughter particularly riveting. It goes without saying that their tale may have been embellished and their shortcomings been exaggerated by gossip, so inevitably some of the printed sources have to be regarded with caution. Nevertheless, it is evident from the most reliable of them that Princess Charlotte was a very lively member of the family – and probably more lively than some of their closest relations may have wished.

At least one fairly recent work, *Purple Secret* (Röhl, Warren & Hunt, 1998), has had the benefit of correspondence from archives which laid bare the problems and the animosity between both women. John Röhl's magnificent three-volume biography of Emperor William has also made full use of other letters from Princess Charlotte. As my reference notes show, I have relied quite heavily on these titles, and I would like to acknowledge my debt to them in particular in the course of my researches.

One day perhaps another biographer will be granted full access to further material. In the meantime, I hope this account will prove of as much interest to those who read it as it was to me when I was writing it.

This work first appeared in electronic form on Amazon Kindle Direct Publishing in 2012. I was astonished at how well it sold in that format, and three years later I am glad to have the opportunity to present a revised, expanded version in paperback as well.

In conclusion, my thanks are due to Kori Roff Lawrence, Sue Woolmans, and many others on the Facebook Royal Books Page – they know who they are - for their help and encouragement; to Sylvia Hemsil for her assistance with proof-reading; and as ever to my wife Kim for her unfailing support and interest.

John Van der Kiste

1
'Definitely not very sensible'
1860-1877

Prince Frederick William of Prussia and Victoria, Princess Royal of Great Britain, were married on 25 January 1858. Their first daughter and second child was born at Neue Palais, Potsdam, on 24 July 1860. Victoria, known in the family as 'Vicky', had been fortunate to survive the birth of her eldest child William. At one stage during what had been a very difficult confinement in January 1859, mother and child were all but given up as past saving. The result was a baby and future German Emperor with a deformed left arm and hand.

Despite this unpromising start to motherhood, very soon after his birth, the princess longed for a second child. She hoped desperately that it would be a perfect son this time, for she was increasingly weary of 'being teased [sic] and tormented with questions, wh[ich]...always seem to me like a reproach'.[1] Fortunately her second pregnancy proved to be trouble-free and had a happier ending. Queen Victoria was thrilled to hear the news, as she wrote effusively from Osborne House in a letter to her daughter the following day:

> Thousand, thousand good wishes, blessings and congratulations! Everything seems to have passed off as easily (indeed more so) as I could have expected though I always thought it would be very easy, and totally different to the last time, and the darling baby – such a fine child. I am delighted it is a little girl, for they are such much [sic] more amusing children.[2]

She added that the young uncles and aunts at Osborne had a half-holiday to celebrate the news, and cooked at the Swiss Cottage.

One week later the Queen thanked her daughter for a 'charming, tasteful locket' and for pieces of her hair; 'The dear little nameless lady seems to have a great quantity of it! How I long to see her!'[3]

The baby was christened Victoria Elizabeth Augusta Charlotte, and throughout her life she was always known by the last of these names in honour of the King's sister, the former Princess Charlotte of Prussia, who had become Empress Alexandra of Russia. After her elder brother's faltering attempts to call her 'dear sister' or 'little sister', she was initially known in the family as 'Ditta'. As an adult, to her cousins, she would generally be called 'Charly'.

Now that Princess Frederick William was also the mother of an apparently perfect daughter, she admitted in a letter to her father that she was very proud of her, 'and feel to care more about her, than I did about the Boy [William] when he was born'.[4]

The name for the new princess had not been chosen without a certain amount of disagreement. Queen Victoria had already expressed some dislike on the part of both herself and the Prince Consort for the names of Elizabeth and Charlotte, which she thought were 'two of the ugliest housemaids' names' she had ever known. Her personal preferences, she let it be known, were for Frederica and Wilhelmina. In view of the Hohenzollerns' fondness for naming nearly all their princes Frederick or William, or perhaps with both names, this was entirely understandable.

Nevertheless her daughter had her way. The Queen said that although she did not admire the name of Charlotte, 'I shall love it for my dear little granddaughter's sake'.[5] She was also pacified to some extent when Vicky agreed that the name Victoria, which she declared ought to be given to all her female descendants, was also included. 'I do hope one of your daughters, if you have any more,' she wrote, 'will be called Victoria, so that there may be 4 generations of Victorias.'[6] She was more accommodating than the embittered Queen Elizabeth of Prussia, who had always thoroughly disliked her British niece by marriage. According to the young mother, she 'was so much displeased at the name that it made her still more cross and ungracious the two times she has been to see me'.[7]

At first, Charlotte was perfection personified in the eyes of her mother. 'She is 1000 times nicer because she is always good and a great deal prettier than [William] ever was and takes twice as much notice now, as he did when he was twice the age she is,' she wrote to Queen Victoria when the bay was only three months old. 'I am so proud of her and like to show her off, which I never did with him as he was so thin and pale and fretful at her age.'[8]

William and Charlotte of Prussia both had the distinction of being the only grandchildren of Queen Victoria born within the lifetime of her husband, the Prince Consort. When he paid what would prove to be his final visit to Coburg for family reasons in the autumn of 1860, it was the only time he would ever be able to see them. Fifteen months later, in December 1861, he took to his bed with what was believed to be typhoid fever, and died on 14 December, aged only forty-two.

The year of 1861, which ended with a death in the family, had opened in similar fashion in Germany. When the long-ailing, childless King Frederick William IV of Prussia died at the beginning of January, he was succeeded by William, the eldest of his brothers. William's only son Frederick William was now Crown Prince, and Victoria therefore became Crown Princess.

In August 1862 she gave birth to a third child and second son, Henry. He was followed by two more brothers, Sigismund and Waldemar, both of whom died in childhood, Sigismund from meningitis at twenty-one months, and Waldemar of diphtheria at eleven years. The family was completed with the arrival of three younger sisters, Victoria, Sophie and Margaret, all of whom lived to maturity.

It was often remarked how the Crown Princess treated her three elder children differently to their younger siblings, being strict and critical with the elder, and more doting with the younger. As a parent she evidently took her cue from her father the Prince Consort, and expected remarkable things from the eldest children. Maybe it was inevitable that she would be disappointed if they did not take after her in interests and intellect, yet she would one day come to realise that her insistence on the highest standards was asking too much, as it had been in the case of the upbringing of her unscholarly eldest brother the Prince of Wales, later King Edward VII. She was less demanding with the three younger daughters, all of whom always adored her. If she had only shown their eldest sister Charlotte more understanding in her earlier years, the relationship between them might have been a happier one. There would always be something of a gulf, particularly in childhood, between the three eldest children and the three youngest daughters, whom William would contemptuously refer to as 'the English colony'. According to one recent biographer, John Röhl, deep down the Crown Princess subconsciously rejected her three eldest children as 'complete Prussians', confessing that at times she felt like a hen who had hatched a brood of ducklings.[9]

Throughout her childhood, Charlotte gave her mother one worry after another. At twenty-one months she was throwing disturbingly violent tantrums, or 'such outbreaks of rage & stubbornness that she screams blue murder'.[10] When she was three years old, the Crown Princess was alarmed by what seemed to be the girl's hyperactive nature, noting that 'her little mind seems almost too active for her body - she is so nervous & sensitive and so quick. Her sleep is not so sound as it should be – and she is so very thin.' A heavy cold she suffered from at around this time, it was thought, had affected her stomach and liver, and she was unwell for a long time afterwards. She remained very skinny as a little girl, and when naked was 'an object for studies in anatomy, nothing but skin and bones'.[11] A year later, the Crown Princess found her 'very sensitive & nervous', 'easily upset', and 'definitely not very sensible'.[12]

Nevertheless she could be very amusing in her remarks, as small children generally were. When she was about three years old her father was away on military service, and one hot summer afternoon her mother was playing outside with the children in the palace gardens. Charlotte asked her mother if she would undress her, as it was very hot and she did so want to be naked. The lady-in-waiting, Lady Walburga Paget, was standing close by. As the sentry was marching past, four-year-old William asked Lady Walburga in a loud voice whether she would also like to run around under the orange trees naked. The Crown Princess was full of admiration for the soldier who managed to keep such a straight face.[13] A year or so later, four-year-old Charlotte remarked to her elder brother that God was in her heart now, and she could feel it. William indignantly remarked that this was impossible, as God was in *his* heart. When she insisted, he told her that he would have Jesus Christ in his.[14]

Sometimes the comments the Crown Princess made on her daughter were less critical and more sympathetic. As she was preparing for a family visit to Balmoral at the end of September 1863, she wrote to the Queen that Ditta was not just still looking very thin, but also ill at ease with unfamiliar faces: 'I hope she will not be shy with you but she is afraid of strangers particularly ladies and it is difficult to make friends with her.'[15]

It never ceased to worry her that her two eldest children were far from physically perfect. The injury to her son was a particularly hard cross to bear. In May 1865, a little strangely, she wrote bitterly to the Queen how hard it should be that her eldest child, being second in line to the throne, had the misfortune of a deformed arm; 'It would not matter with poor Henry or Ditta.'[16]

Just over a year later she was singing the praises of her second daughter, another Victoria, born in April 1866 and aged merely three months, comparing her favourably with the first, who was being 'a little 'silly', and whose intellect was not improving.[17] So far Charlotte was turning out to be 'a most difficult child to bring up, if she were not so stupid and backward her being naughty would not matter.' As if she then realised that she had been too critical, she added that the girl was 'at the moment very pretty'.[18]

The somewhat strange comments did not stop. Forgetting that as a mother she herself had often been too ready to find fault with her eldest daughter, Queen Victoria was concerned lest the Crown Princess should be continually reproaching Charlotte too much, and urged her 'not to speak of her or treat her generally as such a naughty and stupid child - but be very kind and encouraging though severe whenever it is necessary.'[19] This was in response to one of the Crown Princess's letters, complaining that her then eight-year-old daughter was very backward and in educational terms far behind all other little children that she met.

Three years later, her grandmother in Britain was to have first-hand experience of the eleven-year-old girl's naughtiness on a visit to Balmoral in September 1871 when she refused to shake hands with the Highland ghillie John Brown, giving the excuse that 'Mama says I ought not to be too familiar with servants.'[20] In fact her mother, who was sometimes reproached by her family for putting too little distance between servants and herself, was almost certainly not to blame. Charlotte evidently took her cue from her father's side, probably from her grandparents, the German Emperor William and Empress Augusta.

Having been a nervous, agitated child, Charlotte would soon display signs of the behavioural problems that would continue into adult life. She was inclined to suck on and chew her clothing, or bite her fingernails until, it is alleged, her mother tried strapping her hands to her sides or making her wear gloves.[21] The Crown Princess thought that she had inherited the worst of the Hohenzollern looks, and had a long body but very short limbs, giving the appearance of being unnaturally top-heavy when she was standing, but creating the illusion of looking tall when she was seated.

At the same time she was developing a wilful nature. To make matters worse, she and her brother William were thoroughly spoiled by their German grandparents, Emperor William and Empress Augusta, who were inclined to encourage her in her acts of petty rebellion against her parents while she was growing up. Her written letters also gave cause for parental disapproval, as did those of her two eldest brothers. The Crown Princess thought that they were written in a style which was 'indescribably bad for children of 12 & 13 years of age who have enjoyed English instruction all their life',[22] and had very poor handwriting, probably because they were made to write with steel nibs.

When she was about thirteen, Charlotte found a kindred spirit in the family considerably closer to her own age. In January 1874 her maternal uncle Alfred, Duke of Edinburgh, married Grand Duchess Marie Alexandrovna, the sole surviving daughter of Tsar Alexander II of Russia. Marie, who thoroughly disliked England and sorely missed her old home in Russia, was lonely in her new environment and thoroughly ill at ease with most members of her husband's family. Something in her felt sorry for Charlotte; they became close friends, and the latter was ready to worship the Duchess of Edinburgh, forging a relationship which would last until both women died within about a year of each other.

The problems between mother and daughter persisted into the latter's adolescence, partly because the Crown Princess expected rather too much of her, especially where her intellectual development was concerned. In May 1874 she reported to Queen Victoria that the girl had recently improved, was 'gentle and amiable and willing to do all she is told, and much nicer towards the brothers and sisters,' but that she was not clever, and never would be, as she appeared to have few if any interests:

> no taste for learning or reading, for art or natural history, so it is no use to expect these things of her – one cannot force them into existence if there is no natural turn for them; if she only grows up a nice and good girl – and in time becomes trustworthy and conscientious that is all I can expect! Her temper is very even and good now! Unfortunately her nose has remained exactly in the same state as it was when we were at Osborne – like a violent cold in the head! It is too tiresome...She grows so little that you would think she was nine or ten, has not an atom of figure, or waist, and shows no sign of her health beginning to change.[23]

Queen Victoria expressed concern at certain aspects of Charlotte's upbringing, and thought she was being driven too hard with an over-demanding educational regime to which she was unsuited. When the girl was fourteen, the Queen warned her

10

daughter to be careful; 'you are really not doing her good by forcing her on with her lessons for she will not get stronger and not grow if she is overworked.'[24] (Perhaps the Queen belatedly realised how counter-productive the Prince Consort's passion for a scholarly regime for their eldest son Albert Edward, Prince of Wales, had been). Physically Charlotte was so small that, although she was aged nearly fourteen at the time, she still looked just like a child of only nine or ten.

When it came to her eldest daughter's upbringing, the Crown Princess was inclined to be more strict than her husband. In 1875 they gave a magnificent ball at the Neue Palais with the theme of a 'Fete at the Court of the Medici in Florence'. No attention to detail in the costumes was spared, with the Crown Princess wearing a dress of rich crimson velvet, and the Crown Prince in the costume of a Venetian nobleman, complete with velvet plumed hat. Shortly before the ball there was some discussion as to whether Charlotte should be allowed to attend. She begged her parents to give her permission, dressed like her mother as a Princess of the Medici, and as it was a special occasion her father was prepared to agree. But the Crown Princess maintained that girls of fourteen ought to be in bed at that time, and the answer was a gentle no. Nevertheless, as one of the nursery maids would bear witness, Charlotte, her nine-year-old sister Victoria, and seven-year-old Waldemar all crept quietly out of bed and hung over the banisters until quite a late hour to see what they were missing.[25]

2
'An excellent man in his way'
1877-1878

Perhaps it was just as well that, by this time, Charlotte was about to fly the family nest. On 1 April 1877 her engagement to her second cousin Bernhard, Hereditary Prince of Saxe-Meiningen, was formally proclaimed at Berlin. The date had been chosen as it was the twenty-sixth birthday of her husband-to-be.

Bernhard, nine years her senior, had joined the Saxe-Meiningen Infantry Regiment in 1867, and rose to the rank of second lieutenant. Two years later he enrolled at Heidelberg University to study classical philology. His studies were interrupted in 1870 by the outbreak of the Franco-Prussian War, during which he served as an aide with the 6th Thuringian Infantry Regiment, and he was present at the battle of Wörth and the siege of Paris.

After the cessation of hostilities he returned to his studies in Heidelberg and then Leipzig, where he graduated in 1873. Later he took part in military training with the Fusilier Guards Regiment of the Prussian Army in Berlin. But his abiding interest in the Greek language and culture remained a lifelong pursuit; he later wrote several books and published some translations of classical works. Between 1873 and 1894, he also ventured abroad on a number of study trips to Greece and Asia Minor in order to visit archaeological sites and work with well-known archaeologists, who invariably appreciated his expertise and knowledge.

Although contemporaries maintained that there was always something of the German officer about his character, his classical interests marked him out as a man with interests beyond the military. From this point of view the Crown Princess could perhaps have hardly wished for a better son-in-law. In terms of personality, during the years ahead she would not find him so congenial.

He was the eldest son of George II, who had been the reigning Duke of Saxe-Meiningen since 1866, by his first wife, another Charlotte of Prussia, daughter of the Emperor's younger brother Albrecht. George and Charlotte had married in May 1850, when he was twenty-four and she was only eighteen. Although they enjoyed a happy marriage while it lasted, her life was destined to be a sad one. She wholeheartedly shared his love for the arts, being passionate about music and was a composer of several military marches, songs, and piano pieces. However, her health had always been delicate. In January 1855, when she was twenty-three years old, her younger son, two-year-old George, died. At the time she was carrying a third son, who was born in March but only lived for a few hours, and she died in childbirth.

The grieving George was keen to find a second wife, if only as a mother for his motherless son and daughter. In October 1858 he married his second cousin Feodora of Hohenlohe-Langenburg, the youngest daughter of Queen Victoria's elder half-sister Feodora. She lacked the intellectual and artistic interests of his first wife and showed no interest in acquiring any. George did his best to put this right, with the full approval of his mother-in-law, who noted that it was 'very sensible of him indeed to arrange for his bride to be much occupied with lessons, to take drawing lessons, and to hear lectures on history'.[1] They had three sons, two of whom lived to maturity, but the youngest, born in May 1865, only lived for three days.

Feodora soon came to realise with sadness that her husband had never really ceased to pine for his first wife. She was never happy at Meiningen, and above all she realised that at best she would never be much more than a poor substitute for the cultured Charlotte. After the death of their youngest son, she stayed away from the duchy as much as possible. In January 1872 she fell ill with scarlet fever. Although they had not been well suited, George was very fond of her, was deeply upset when she became ill, and sent regular telegrams on her condition to his mother-in-law. Nevertheless, she died the following month, aged only thirty-two.

Thirteen months after her death, in March 1873, George married for the third time. His new wife was Ellen Franz, a former actress, who was given the style Baroness von Heldburg, although as she was not of noble birth she could never become Duchess of Saxe-Meiningen. It was a morganatic marriage which incurred the wrath of Emperor William, who had been closely related to him by marriage as his first wife had been his niece. The Duke remained a close friend of Emperor William, although relations between them were strained by the Duke's third marriage. The Emperor was displeased that the former husband of a Prussian princess, now a widower twice over, should not have thought twice about marrying beneath him, although he was later forgiven.

Bernhard was likewise angered by his father taking a wife of lesser rank, and threatened to appeal directly to the people of Meiningen, believing that he would have their support. Although ministers and officials at the duchy court agreed with him, and some resigned their offices in protest, the majority of people in the duchy were fully prepared to accept her as their Duke's chosen wife. An angry George became furious with anybody who would not recognise or treat her as his equal, especially when the army refused to salute her. He even sent a representative to the court of Berlin, addressing Emperor William with an official complaint, but the only response to this was that Prussian officers should salute her as Baroness, and no more. Duke George and his Baroness did not have any children, but like his first wife, she shared his love of the arts and theatre in Meiningen, and it proved a very happy union which endured until his death forty-one years later. Both of them, with Ludwig Chronegk, the director of the court theatre at Saxe-Meiningen, spared no effort to make it one of the most forward-looking acting companies in Germany, with all three taking an active interest in appropriate scenery and costumes for all productions, and the education of young theatrical students.

Unlike his father Bernhard, who had abdicated as Duke under pressure from the German Chancellor Otto von Bismarck after siding with the defeated Austrians during the Six Weeks' War in 1866, George II had remained loyal to the Prussians and was made a Lieutenant General in the Prussian army. During the Franco-Prussian War, he had led two regiments of soldiers from Meiningen and captured the first French flags at the battle of Wörth in August 1870, a decisive German victory, as well as fighting in nearly every subsequent battle during the conflict. He was a member of King William of Prussia's staff when the latter entered Paris. Father and son were both among the gathering of German dukes and princes who witnessed the imperial proclamation at the Salle des Glaces, Versailles, on 18 January 1871, at which King William of Prussia was elevated to the style of German Emperor.

The Duke was a liberal, and a strong supporter of causes such as parliamentary government along British lines, reforms to the legal system, the franchise, and equal rights for women. Because of this, he would find himself out of sympathy with the conservatively-minded Emperor William II, and indeed with his less progressively-inclined son and heir Bernhard.

Despite his reactionary politics, Bernhard was more cultured than the average German army officer. In spite of this he was not regarded by all as the most eligible of husbands. According to a contemporary observer,

> though an excellent man in his way, [Bernhard] was very far from meeting the requirements of the "Prince Charmant" fit to be mated to a princess so gay and so brilliant as Charlotte of Hohenzollern. His appearance is effeminate, his manner finicky and old-maidish to a degree. He is neither stalwart nor good-looking; he excels neither as a dancer nor as a rider, nor yet as an athlete, and he gives one at first sight the impression of being an artist or a composer.[2]

Moreover he was regarded as weak-willed, and the kind of man who would easily be dominated by any wife with a mind of her own. (This would quite possibly be something of an advantage to any princess whom he was to marry, for her at least). He had been invited one day to accompany his cousins Charlotte and William on a switchback railway ride on the Isle of Peacocks in the Pfaueninsel, Berlin's pleasure park. When William accelerated the controls for a joke, his temporarily terrified sister clung to Bernhard, who was sitting next to her. If it was not quite love at first sight, then romance soon followed this initial encounter.

Alternatively it was surely in part a reaction to her mother's constant criticism and marriage was the best, if not the only, means of finding her independence by escaping from her parents' home. The Crown Princess was ever critical of her seventeen-year-old daughter, who she thought was very short and stout; 'she has an immense bust and arms - a long waist and neck, and looks like a big person when she is sitting - and when she gets up she has no legs almost. Unfortunately she is most ungraceful when she moves and walks, sticks out her elbows and trundles about...' In addition, the Crown Princess added unflatteringly, the girl had 'her Papa's hands and feet which for a young girl is most unfortunate.'[3]

Such shortcomings would have counted for less if only she had been a more affectionate daughter. But she and her two eldest brothers all too often gave the impression of being cold and ungrateful, with a lack of feeling which distressed her mother. In a mood of despair, a few weeks after Charlotte's seventeenth birthday, she poured her heart out to Queen Victoria:

> The 3 eldest have not an idea of what their Mama did & suffered for them continually. Few except those immediately around me know what I have gone through for them, the fight, the difficulties, the putting up with characters & treatment wh[ich] I hardly think anybody else would have borne, & which I certainly never could stand again. I have not reaped much gratitude, & have often been bitterly disappointed... The 3 eldest are such complete Prussians in their nature that there is little resemblance with me.[4]

At the same time, over the preceding few months, Charlotte had developed a reputation throughout Berlin for flirtatiousness, malicious gossip and troublemaking. Her anxious mother was often saddened by what she called

> that pretty exterior - & the empty inside, those dangerous character traits! Everyone is initially enthralled, & yet those who know her better know how she really is - and can have neither love nor trust nor respect! It is too sad. There is nothing to be done, it is just a fact, & one can only hope that time & life will serve as teachers to her, & that the good Bernhard will protect & guide her. Then at least her wicked qualities will not be able to cause her any harm.

The Crown Princess's friend at court, Princess Catherine Radziwill, considered that Charlotte was a foolish and frivolous girl who could not really have been in love with anyone at the time. It was her view that she was simply marrying because it was a golden opportunity to escape from a family life which she found becoming increasingly irksome. Nevertheless, the Crown Princess was convinced that her mischievous, perhaps even flighty daughter needed to settle down, and a good husband ought to be just the answer. If Bernhard was not exactly the strong-willed partner that a wayward princess like Charlotte badly needed to keep her in order, with his own intellectual interests he might perhaps succeed in broadening her rather limited horizons.

The engagement lasted almost a year, and at intervals the Crown Princess complained that they were resenting 'the slightest restraint put upon them & Bernhard thinks they ought to do just as they like.'[6] She was also disappointed that her husband the Crown Prince who, as in the case of the costume ball, tended to take a more relaxed view of these things than she did and was prepared to let the young couple go their own way, felt it unnecessary to intervene. However, she had an ally in Queen Victoria, who shared her opinion. The latter likewise deprecated what she and her daughter saw as an unwelcome lapse in standards, declaring that young people had 'lost all modesty for not only do they go about driving, walking & <u>visiting</u> – everywhere <u>alone</u>, they have also <u>now</u> taken to go out everywhere in society ' and were 'getting very American, I fear in their views and ways.'[7]

During the months leading up to the wedding, the Crown Princess particularly enjoyed the task of assembling a trousseau for her daughter, which she wanted 'to be as nice and as useful as possible'. She wrote to Queen Victoria as she prepared it how she vividly remembered the trouble her own mother had taken over hers some twenty years ago, 'and how it touched me that you should see into each little detail yourself.'[8]

Charlotte and Bernhard were married on 18 February 1878 in the chapel at the Berlin Schloss. It was a double ceremony, for on that same day another Hohenzollern bride, Elizabeth Anna, the second daughter of Prince Frederick Charles, one of the Emperor's younger brothers, was marrying Frederick Augustus, later Grand Duke of Oldenburg. The Crown Princess noted afterwards that her daughter 'really looked very pretty – in the silver moiré train, the lace – the orange and myrtle and the veil'.[9]

Among the guests from outside Germany who had come to the ceremonies were King Leopold II and Queen Marie-Henriette of the Belgians, the Prince of Wales and his younger brother Arthur, Duke of Connaught, who would marry a Prussian princess himself just over a year later. According to the Prince of Wales, who was always ready with a tactful compliment, the bride looked 'like a fresh little rose'.[10] Maybe the Prince of Wales had seen something of a kindred spirit in his high-spirited Prussian niece. Both of them had refused to a certain extent to conform with the advanced intellectual standards wished on them by one if not both parents. The elder one had already discovered, as would the younger, that marriage would undoubtedly mean a measure of emancipation and the liberty to indulge in a less rigidly-controlled social life. One sadly noted absence from the festivities was that of the Crown Princess's sister Alice, Grand Duchess of Hesse and the Rhine, who was unable to come for reasons of ill-health.[11]

It proved to be an unusually mild and sunny day for the time of year. *The Times* correspondent in Berlin noted poetically that 'Nature, too, smiles upon the rare event, and by inverting the seasons, creates a summer's day in February.'[11]

The 'solemnities' began with the signing of the marriage contracts in the palace and the civil marriage ceremonies, attended only by the closest relatives. After that the royal and imperial family and their guests gathered in the chapel adjoining the palace, with about sixty members of reigning families present, where the brides freely mingled with the throng. At 6.30 in the evening the coronets worn by the brides were brought into the room by the officers of the royal treasury, escorted by life guards and palace grenadiers. When the Empress had fastened the coronets on to the brides' heads, the Emperor gave the signal for the procession to form and proceed to the chapel, with the marshals and chamberlains of the court opening the cortege. After them walked the bridal couples, attended by their ladies and gentlemen-in-waiting. Preceded by several court functionaries and 'an imposing army of generals', the next royalties were the Emperor, with the Queen of the Belgians on his right and Elizabeth, Grand Duchess of Oldenburg, on his left. Ladies-in-waiting and maids of honour came next, followed by the Crown Prince and Princess, and remaining royalties in turn. As the procession slowly advanced through the halls and the picture gallery to the chapel, it was said by *The Times* to form 'a brilliant picture', with the ladies' magnificent dresses and their long trains vying with the ermine of the principal male personages and jewellery. 'Like dark specks in these waving floods of *drap d'or*, velvet satin, and silk appeared the gentlemen in their comparatively sober array of Prussian blue, relieved by sparkling ribands, sashes, and Orders. As usual in these Prussian assemblies, there was no lack of feminine grace and masculine beauty.'[13]

The procession then entered the chapel, where the congregation, including field marshals and knights of the Black Eagle, members of the federal and privy councils, military officers and others were assembled. The bridal couples took up their station in front of the altar, while the imperial family and chief royal guests ranged themselves in a circle round them. The chaplain delivered a short address, then read the liturgy and the couples made their vows. As they exchanged rings, the roar of artillery announced the tidings to the people of Berlin, while the parents and grandparents offered their congratulations to both couples.

Next the royalties moved to the Red Velvet Chamber, accompanied by the sound of 'sacred music', where further congratulations were offered. Following a short interval, the Emperor and Empress proceeded to the White Hall and ascended a dais in front of the throne. Surrounded by the family and guests, a signal was given for *'la cour'* in which the whole assembly paraded past the throne, bowing to Emperor William and Empress Augusta, with the brides and grooms, and the German ambassadors' wives, Lady Odo Russell and Countess Karolyi, leading the procession, followed by the wives of the various envoys and secretaries. After them came the wives of the German dignitaries, preceded by Princess Bismarck. They were followed by the gentlemen, in an apparently endless file.

Supper came next, with royalties in the Knights' Hall, while the guests had buffets in a whole suite of apartments of the palace. At the royal table princes and dukes handed soup tureens around and poured out the wine. Perhaps the most spectacular items at the supper to be seen were two towering wedding cakes from England which had been ordered specially by the Crown Princess, and much admired by the guests who had apparently never seen anything like them before. When the soup was removed, the Emperor gave the toast, 'Abiding happiness to the newly-married couples.'

The festivities lasted for over six hours, and again according to the Crown Princess, 'it was <u>very very</u> long – <u>very</u> hot, <u>very</u> tiring, and almost too serious, solemn and heavy for a wedding, but so it always is here.'[14] One fact not remarked on at the time, but a disquieting sign of things to come with regard to her state of health, was that the bride fainted three times that day with sheer exhaustion. Like her mother, she was not strong enough to cope with the extremes of heat and standing around at such formal gatherings.[15]

The day concluded with a *Fackeltanz*, or torch dance. The word dance was evidently something of a misnomer, for according to *The Times*, 'a more formal, un-terpsichorean dance cannot well be imagined.'[16] At midnight, after a given signal the music, a polonaise composed for the occasion, began to play as the Master of the Household entered the hall, carrying his wand of office. He was preceded by two rows of Prussian cabinet ministers, all carrying large torches and walking around the room in time to the music, bowing before the newly married couples, seated on a raised dais next to Their Majesties. The brides and grooms, attended by ladies carrying the brides' trains, then stepped down to follow the torchbearers as they processed around the room. After this each bride in turn took the Emperor by one hand and her nearest male relative the other, while the grooms took the Empress and the bride's mothers, and all of them walked slowly around the room in time to the music. This continued until the brides had paraded with each of the princes and the grooms with each of the princesses, with each group curtseying to the Emperor and Empress, and it involved no less than twenty-two circuits altogether.

According to Charlotte's younger sister Victoria, who was aged eleven at the time, the effect was 'really very charming and fascinating, though decidedly tiring for the bride and bridegroom'.[17] After several hours of marriage ceremonies throughout the day, it was probably equally tiring for the rest of the guests and household as well.

Once this was completed the exhausted Crown Princess helped her daughter to her room. After helping her to bed, she felt utterly desolate, and gave full vent to her feelings in a letter to Queen Victoria how she:

> with an <u>aching</u> heart left her, <u>no</u> more <u>mine</u> now – to care for & watch & take care of but <u>another's</u>, and that is a hard wrench for a mother. With pangs of pain we bring them into this world, with bitter pain we resign them to others for life, to independence – and to shift for themselves. We bore the one for their sakes and with pleasure – and so must we the other.[18]

When she came back later and took a look at her daughter's empty room and bed, 'where <u>every</u> night I have kissed her before lying down myself....I felt very miserable.'[19]

3
'Nature has made her so'
1878-1888

Charlotte and Bernhard began their married life in a small villa near the Neue Palais at Potsdam, formerly the home of Princess Leignitz, the second and morganatic wife of King Frederick William III. He had died in 1840 and she remained there in widowhood until her death in 1873. The Crown Princess had arranged the furnishings for her daughter and son-in-law, and she looked forward to being able to keep a friendly eye on them. This was what Charlotte did not want, as she was well aware that as long as she remained in Potsdam she and Bernhard would never have any independence. Nevertheless she was aware that as a married woman she would have greater freedom to go her own way, and she would be impervious to any further parental criticism or efforts to control her.

Later that year, accompanied by Prince William and with a British diplomat of German ancestry in attendance on them, husband and wife paid a strictly incognito visit to Paris. Feelings about anything and anyone German still ran high throughout France within the first few years of her defeat in the war of 1870-71, and it would have not been wise for Charlotte to make her presence as granddaughter of the conquering German Emperor obvious. While many members of the German imperial family refused to have any more to do with republican France than was strictly necessary, Charlotte and Bernhard were among the minority who, like many British and Russian royals, adored the French capital, no matter what the country's political complexion might be. Among other attractions, they saw the great hall at Versailles where her grandfather had been proclaimed Emperor, went on a balloon ride from the Tuileries, visited Bagatelle, the home of Sir Richard Wallace, filled with art treasures which would later go on display in the Wallace Collection in London, and attended the opera where they saw a performance of *The Queen of Sheba*. They avoided going to restaurants, and generally dined every evening in their apartment at l'Hotel Chatham.

By the autumn Charlotte knew that she was expecting a child. On 12 May 1879 she gave birth to a daughter who was given the names Feodora Victoria Augusta Marie Marianne, and always known by the name Feodora. This baby was the Crown Princess's first grandchild and also Queen Victoria's first great-grandchild.

At the time the Crown Princess was in deep mourning for the prince who would have been the baby's eleven-year-old uncle, the Crown Princess's beloved youngest son Waldemar. An irrepressible, lovable young scamp full of personality, he had been adored by the whole family who tragically died of diphtheria about six weeks earlier, on 27 March, a loss that had almost broken her spirit for good. Close friends said that she was never quite the same woman again. 'The grief of my parents for the loss of this splendid son was unspeakable,' his eldest brother William wrote, 'our pain deep and cruel beyond words. All I could do for my departed brother was to hold all night vigil in the Friedenskirche.'[1] Totally shattered by her bereavement, following so soon after the death from the same disease of her favourite sister Alice, Grand Duchess of Hesse and the Rhine, her joy at the birth of a first grandchild was tempered with an irrational but arguably understandable sense of outrage that another human being should be given life when 'my own Waldie has been taken'.[2] Under the circumstances, for a contemporary biographer to write that the news 'came just when the hearts of the sorrowing family most needed her sweet ministrations'[3] perhaps did not ring altogether true.

Charlotte was also deeply affected by the death of her youngest brother, and relations between mother and daughter did improve for a while. A letter from the Crown Princess to Queen Victoria, written a few weeks after her daughter's nineteenth birthday, mingled reproach and disappointment with a measure of understanding and passive acceptance of the faults which she knew were too ingrained to change:

> I fear where most people only see her pretty face – and are taken with her amicable exterior. – She <u>has</u> the wish to be amicable & make herself pleasant, but the poor Child can never be a help mate or a resource to any one. I admit it is not her fault. Nature has made her so – and education <u>cannot</u> do

all! Education cannot give either capabilities of the mind nor a thoroughly good kind warm heart! – This is a great trial....She is very independent, and very obstinate, so one cannot influence her, as one w[oul]d wish'.[4]

At about this time Charlotte and her German grandmother, the sharp-tongued Empress Augusta, had a conversation in which the latter, it was said, asked after the Crown Princess and asked if Charlotte had heard from her, 'with a scornful laugh & a sarcastic tone'. Charlotte was sympathetic enough to admit being 'pained & shocked at the way in which she inquired after [the Crown Princess]'.[5] When the Crown Prince learnt of this, he found his mother's attitude similarly difficult to comprehend, but conceded that there was nothing they could do until she calmed down.

Even so, despite her rebellious nature, Charlotte was still fond of her mother and sometimes saddened at the estrangement between her and her elder brother. She went to some effort to try and mend the rift between them. It saddened her that he 'should again have been so unkind & neglectful' towards their mother, and thought it was all the fault of his childhood tutors Georg Hinzpeter and Octavie Darcourt, who were later married to each other. Between them, Charlotte maintained, the couple 'quite mismanaged us, & a thing I can never forgive them, turned Willy's loving feelings from his Parents, & said all sorts of unkind untruthes [sic] of you, to try & get him round'.[6] She was pleasantly surprised to note how affectionate he could be with his baby niece, noting that she 'never saw him so nice before & [he] played so dearly with Feo who was beside herself, & laughed so merrily.'[7]

About three weeks later she was writing reassuringly to her mother that she really thought he did not mean to be so unkind and thoughtless as he often appeared to be;

> he never shows much feeling, but I think he feels very much & I have often in these last days heard him speak so nicely of you; I have often spoke[n] right out to him & told him [my] mind about his behaviour to you & he seemed quite astonished, that I said he was not like a good son; a man can never to my mind feel like a daughter does towards a mother; they don't know what it is to bring a child into the world.[8]

When he was married and had children himself, Charlotte concluded, then he would surely understand what it was to be grateful to one's parents. Although her relations with her own daughter would often be extremely stormy, it was apparent that as a young mother she was devoted to the child, and motherhood had almost certainly mellowed her feelings towards her own mother, if only for a while.

A few days later, Charlotte told the Crown Princess that she had had a long conversation with William about his behaviour to her, and shown him one of their mother's letters in which she complained of his lack of feeling. She assured the Crown Princess that he did not mean to behave badly to her, and 'said he loved you quite as much as any of us, & I am certain that he does; only that he does not know how to show it'.[9] A day later, 'with the best intentions' but also with an astonishing lack of foresight, Charlotte showed him all their mother's letters in which she had complained in detail of his unfilial behaviour and set out her grievances against him. Such correspondence had clearly been meant for the eyes of the recipient alone. She said that he was quite upset when he read them, intended to write to their mother in order to make everything up with her, and beg her not to be angry with him:

It does seem so sad to see the eldest of the family not getting on with his Parents; & I trust my own Mother you won't be angry with me, for having behaved as I have done, but I did not like to let the old year end & the new one begin, without Nigger [William] making up to you & turning over a new leave [sic] so that you should not have to complain about him any more.'[10]

The Crown Princess feared that it would make him angry with her, as his conscience did not tell him how offensively he was behaving, or how little gratitude for and trust in her he was showing. As she feared, the only result was a letter from him which has not survived but in which, as was evident from her reply to him which has survived, no reconciliation had been brought about. She found the tone of it 'thoroughly disrespectful', and remarked although she was glad that he was friends with his sister, his duty to his mother surely came first. She complained to the Crown Prince of their eldest daughter's 'indiscretion', which she considered 'foolish & mischievous', but this seemed to rankle less with her than William's 'inappropriate & unseemly' attitude towards her. Even so, Charlotte's well-intentioned but less than diplomatic attempts to build bridges between mother and son had clearly failed.

26

Ironically, early in December 1879, while this correspondence was in progress, the Crown Princess had been writing to her husband of her hopes that the good-natured but plain and pious Princess Augusta ('Dona') of Schleswig-Holstein would have a favourable effect on Charlotte's 'dangerous' character.[11] By this time it was increasingly likely that this was the princess whom William would marry. It had long been clear that as an adult Charlotte was growing apart from William, thinking him too immature and too young to know what he was doing, cold-hearted and incapable of being in love with anyone. At the same time she thought her brother-in-law Ernest was in love with Dona and had ideas about marrying her himself. In spite of this, she had a very low opinion of Dona, whom she considered in a letter to her mother to be 'silent, barely communicative and very shy', especially in comparison with her 'bright-eyed' younger sister Caroline Matilda.[12] It therefore seemed a little strange that she should wish the girl as a wife to Bernhard's brother instead.

William was quick to repay his sister's hostility in kind. In May 1880 he and Dona planned to go for a drive together, something which was regarded as thoroughly improper in the case of a young couple who were merely betrothed and not married. Charlotte intended, or was asked, to accompany them or at least follow them in a second carriage. When William was told he refused to hear of it, or in his own words, consider taking 'an elephant' along with them.[13]

The Crown Princess was particularly annoyed that Charlotte was behaving 'more than coolly' towards her future sister-in-law, and seemed to be going around whipping up feelings against her. The Crown Prince was well aware of his son's faults and inclined to share his eldest daughter's reservations. Even so, once the betrothal was officially announced that summer, he was so alarmed by Charlotte's cold behaviour towards Dona and her attempts to stir up feeling against her among the 'smart set' that he had to take her aside and warn her 'where it would lead if our daughter from the outset turned against her brother & sister-in-law in this way, instead of lovingly embracing them.'[14] Bernhard also heartily disliked Dona, with whom he had nothing in common. He claimed that she was tactless, stupid and almost illiterate. As Dona never made any pretensions to sharing the fashionable modern lifestyle which he and his wife eagerly embraced, she never had anything in common with the Saxe-Meiningens, and never would have.

Ironically, time would prove the cynical Charlotte and Bernhard to be better judges of character. Not long after the marriage of William and Augusta Victoria in February 1881, the Crown Prince and Princess would find that their verdicts had been correct. Dona showed herself to be small-minded, empty-headed, and xenophobic. These were the last qualities they wanted in a daughter-in-law, particularly one whom they hoped might have been a suitable influence on William, instead of reinforcing his less likeable prejudices.

The rift between the sisters-in-law, who were so different in personality, would never be healed. If Charlotte thought Dona was a sanctimonious, colourless bore, the traditional obedient little German *hausfrau*, Dona found her sister-in-law a shallow, scheming social butterfly. Both women were always ready to make fun of each other behind their backs. These damning opinions of each were shared by several who knew them, although they were naturally too careful to say so. At the silver wedding celebrations of the Crown Prince and Princess, their children staged a *tableau vivant*, similar to those which the young Princess Royal had often done with her brothers and sisters for the benefit of their own parents many years before. The heavily pregnant Dona missed a vital cue at the performance and was effortlessly upstaged by her sister-in-law, who made a good amateur actress, effortlessly stole the limelight[15] and did not attempt to conceal her disdain of the poor showing the elder woman made beside her.

The Crown Princess was still finding her relationship with Charlotte difficult, and regularly wrote of her anxieties to Queen Victoria. 'I shall burn what you say about Charlotte,' the latter wrote in reply in March 1880 to one such letter. 'Married children are very often a great trial at first but one gets accustomed to their follies as time goes on and many things right themselves. Still it is very wrong of young people not to listen and take advice for they have no experience'.[16] The Crown Princess was evidently anxious that this was one of her letters which should not be preserved for posterity. In October 1881, eighteen months later, the Queen found herself once again trying to act as peacemaker, taking her gently to task for expecting the young woman to share her enthusiasm for art and architecture. 'You are rather severe on Charlotte,' she wrote to her daughter. 'I don't consider myself "uneducated" and yet I could not live in churches, the frescos and galleries as you do.'[17]

The Crown Princess soon became devoted to her first grandchild. By July 1880 she was singing the little girl's praises so much in her letters to England that Queen Victoria was moved to say she found it rather excessive. She told her daughter that 'as regards the baby I think you are hardly a fair judge. Hardly anyone I know has such a *culte* for little babies as you have.'[18]

Like Queen Victoria, Feodora's mother never shared this *culte* for babies. She thoroughly resented the whole business of being pregnant, as it had severely restricted the freedom and lifestyle which she had craved and thought was hers by right once she was married. Now she proved herself to be very unmaternal, and declared to her own mother's dismay that she had absolutely no intention of having any more children.

Not long after the pregnancy, she went back to the Berlin social round with all its endless opportunities for gossip and mischief. When Bernhard was transferred to a regiment in Berlin her grandfather, Emperor William, gave him and Charlotte a villa near the Tiergarten. This became a centre for smart society, where the ladies met to go skating, riding, holding dinner parties and gossiping while their husbands went out shooting. Charlotte bought all her clothes in Paris, and her sense of style was much admired by her friends and by smart society in general. In addition to this she smoked, drank and developed a reputation for being a gossip by pretending to be a friend to someone, gaining their confidence, then using the information against them at any later opportunity which might present itself.

Charlotte was well liked by some sections of her society as a society hostess whose soirées were always entertaining. She was also regarded sympathetically by those who disliked the Crown Princess and thought that she had been an unnecessarily demanding mother to her eldest children. The eldest daughter, they considered, was the most attractive, the most stylish, and the most interesting in terms of personality. They thought that she easily outshone her younger sisters who were looked down on as homely, 'absolutely deficient in feminine elegance or chic, and, while accomplished, are extremely dull, and not a bit sparkling or witty.'[19] Other observers might have regarded the newly-married Hereditary Princess as an acid-tongued woman whom they would cross at their peril.

With her love of outrageous and sarcastic comments she soon became the centre of Berlin's fast set, or in the parlance of a later age something of a 'wild child'. Her paternal grandmother, Empress Augusta, had a special place for this young woman who so enjoyed passing on tittle-tattle, even if some of it was directed against her own family.

Relations between sister and brother did not improve, and Charlotte may have reproached herself a little for her apparent clumsiness and lack of discretion. Less than two years later, she was writing to their mother of her displeasure with William and how sorry she was that he had not found the time to write to her; 'I think it very heartless & unkind of him'.[20] To Herman, Prince of Hohenlohe-Langenburg, she described her brother as 'more childish [and] egotistical than ever'.[21] A couple of weeks later, she wrote to him again complaining of William's behaviour towards their parents which she said was 'quite horrid & both are in absolute despair in this regard; I neither can nor wish to describe in writing all that has transpired, but I can assure you that Wilhelm is still nothing more than a spoiled, conceited baby.'[22]

Two months later, the situation seemed to be even worse. Charlotte was distressed at 'a number of appalling scenes' between William and his father, the result of his lack of consideration towards his mother. Just seeing the Crown Prince made her 'quite miserable, [for] I was so beside myself at Papa's appearance, he was literally ill with rage!'[23]

Contrary to the assertions of some biographers, Charlotte was to find herself on her parents' side again at least part of the time in the bitter quarrels which divided the family from 1885 onwards when Prince Alexander of Battenberg, Prince of Bulgaria, was proposed as a husband for her sister Victoria. Perhaps it was partly a reflection of the growing distance between her and her brother, but she was particularly incensed when William and Dona were so rude towards Queen Victoria. 'What grieved & shocked me beyond all, is Willy's behaviour!' she wrote to her mother. 'Really I have no words, & feel ashamed to think he dared behave in this way to his Grandmama, who has always been kindness itself to him since his birth....When I think *how* kind & generous Yr Mama was to him & to Dona when *they* were engaged & when they were married; no really it is too bad'.[24]

It may or may not have been coincidence that at the end of the previous year Charlotte had been very ill again. She was advised to leave Berlin for somewhere warmer and spent part of the winter at Cannes. The Crown Princess was particularly sympathetic to her plight. In the first week of January 1885 she reported to her sister-in-law Louise, Duchess of Connaught, on her slow improvement after a bout of severe sickness:

She had a thorough malaria poisoning, & consequent anaemia to a high degree, - and it is very difficult to get her round.

Every one of the organs were starved - & the formation of her blood had become a false one. - But I am quite satisfied as to her treatment & hope she will recover altogether. – She cannot walk yet – and only leaves her Bed at 12 in the day! But the neuralgia, fainting and nausea have left her, wh[ich] is a great deal gained![25]

Once she had the chance to get to know her properly, Queen Victoria also became very fond of her first great-grandchild. At the Golden Jubilee celebrations in June 1887 taking place in London, most members of the German imperial family were invited. Among them were the Crown Prince and Crown Princess, William and Dona, Charlotte, Bernhard and Feodora, who was eight years old at the time. Most of the adults stayed at Buckingham Palace while Feodora and her two-year-old cousin Alice, daughter of Prince and Princess Louis of Battenberg, were accommodated at Whitehall in the care of the Queen's Mistress of the Robes, the Duchess of Buccleuch. During the festivities at Windsor Castle the Queen wrote to the Crown Princess that Charlotte was coming to dinner one night 'and sweet little Feo, who is so good and I think grown so pretty. We were delighted to have her and I think the dear child has enjoyed herself.'[26] 'Sweet little Feo' could be seen prominently in the large Jubilee portrait by the Danish court painter Laurits Tuxen of the Queen and her family at Windsor Castle, a girl sitting in the right-hand corner with fair hair falling over her shoulders, the Queen on her right and the Crown Princess in a red dress on her left. Charlotte and Bernhard were part of the group, albeit less conspicuously, the former behind Queen Victoria and the latter in the right-hand corner.

Although relations with her mother were slowly mending a little, Charlotte had not really changed. At heart she remained the most fickle of allies, proving herself an undependable family ally by all too often taking the side of her brother in the unhappy family drama which was about to unfolded around her father's illness. During the winter of 1886 Crown Prince Frederick William had been troubled by a persistent cold and sore throat, which failed to improve by the following spring. An examination by the German doctors revealed a growth on the vocal cord which ultimately proved to be the first sign of cancer of the larynx. Dr Morell Mackenzie, who was summoned to Berlin to examine him and put in charge of the case, recommended that if his patient came to London for the celebrations, he would be able to continue treating him there over the summer.

When her parents went to London for the Golden Jubilee celebrations the previous summer, Charlotte and Bernhard sided with William in saying that it was their mother's fault that William and Dona had been prevented from taking their rightful places as the official representatives of the Hohenzollerns there. Charlotte was not responsible for these accusations, her mother insisted. She believed that the blame lay with William, who had been intent on petty revenge 'for having had to submit to his own dear father going before him on every occasion last year.'[27]

The Crown Prince was advised to avoid Berlin during the winter. After he and the Crown Princess left Balmoral that summer they went to southern Europe and eventually to the Villa Zirio, San Remo, in order to avoid the worst of the Berlin winter. Charlotte herself would also absent herself increasingly from the capital for health reasons in the years ahead. In November the Crown Prince's health took a turn for the worse, and Dr Mackenzie had to admit what the German doctors and many others had believed all along, namely that he was suffering from cancer and probably had only a few months to live. Charlotte was among the family visitors who came to call on her parents there, saddened and moved by the tragic spectacle of an imperial heir who might well be denied his ultimate inheritance for which he had waited so long by predeceasing his father.

4

'An exceedingly fascinating and intelligent woman' 1888-1891

By the time Emperor William died in Berlin on 9 March 1888, aged ninety, his son and successor was a dying man. Now unable to speak above a hoarse whisper, he was reduced to communicating with others by writing everything he wished to say on a pad of paper. Emperor Frederick III, the title he chose for himself, survived his father to reign for only ninety-nine pitiful days.

With the accession to the throne of Emperor William II on 15 June 1888, Charlotte's close relationship to the sovereign as his eldest sister made her much sought-after in Berlin court circles. She was present at the ceremonial opening of the Reichstag in the White Hall of the Stadtschloss in Berlin ten days later, where she was seated next to the six-year-old Crown Prince William and the heavily pregnant Empress, dressed in black as were all the other ladies present. The widowed Empress, who now took the style of Empress Frederick, was very annoyed that Charlotte had attended, despite being in mourning, and denounced as 'very silly and absurd and out of place' the 'pageant and pomp' of the event.[1]

At pains to ingratiate herself with the new regime of her brother, she was not universally trusted. On her twenty-eighth birthday her mother wrote with insight that 'this poor child has always caused us more concern than happiness, she was indescribably difficult to educate, & unfortunately nature has given her a difficult & unhappy character with many qualities that are dangerous for <u>herself</u> as well as for others!'[2] She spared no efforts in making herself indispensable as the bearer of court gossip, and her younger brother Henry, who also regarded her as unreliable, used to call her 'Charley the Pretender' behind her back. To her English cousins, she cheerfully signed herself 'Charlotte the Brat'.

During the first few years of her widowhood, the Empress Frederick was particularly distressed at her eldest son's behaviour, completely in the hands of Bismarck and his colleagues, and at how not only the Emperor but also Charlotte and Henry were unaware of how they were being used. To Queen Victoria, she wrote that they did not understand politics or care about them, and unthinkingly 'join the general cry of the circles in which they moved, & support William with all the roughness & violence of his disposition.'[3]

In 1889 Charlotte gained another close family friend. Her uncle Alfred, Duke of Edinburgh, whose days of active naval service were now over, came to settle at Coburg to await his succession to the little German duchy once his ageing uncle Ernest died, which he did in 1893. Although he was appointed Commander-in-Chief at Devonport and took up his three-year post the following year, from this time onwards he was spending most of his time in Coburg, as well as being based at London and in the west country from time to time.

The Duchess of Edinburgh, who had never made any secret of her dislike of England and her inability to get on with her husband's family, had been very glad to move to Germany with her son and daughters. As she found the capital of the duchy rather too dull, small and provincial for her tastes, Charlotte was pleased to invite her to the villa in Berlin. With her came her two elder daughters Marie, or 'Missy', and Victoria Melita, or 'Ducky'.

For a pen portrait of Charlotte at this time, one is indebted to the memoirs of the younger Marie, who as Queen Dowager of Roumania recalled towards the end of her life:

> Charly, as we called our cousin, was an exceedingly fascinating and intelligent woman. She was small and inclined to be plump (a tendency which she always fought, much to the detriment of her health, for she was nearly always ailing) and she was one of the few women of those days who wore short hair. She was neat to a degree and always beautifully dressed....Never have I heard a softer or more melodious voice; there was a purr in it which would have disarmed an ogre. She was an inveterate smoker and always diffused around her a delicate odour of cigarettes and Hammon. Not really a beauty, her face was most attractive, the lower part having a slight twist, and when she talked, the tip of her small well shaped nose moved slightly downward...Her movements were delicate and quite like those

of a cat, like a cat also the soft way she touched things; each of her gestures was a caress...She knew many things although not as many as she gave you to believe...she spoke always as a connoisseur, be it about horses, music, flowers, cooking or army equipment, and for many long years I bowed down before her superior knowledge till I discovered what she really was.[4]

Reading between the lines in this description, it is clear that Charlotte was not the most pleasant or indeed reliable of friends or relations, as Marie would later find out to her cost. The German Emperor's sister, her younger cousin said, played a large part in her life, and not always a happy one. She related one occasion when she and her sister Victoria Melita were invited to stay with her at her home in Berlin. They had been looking forward to the occasion for a long time, but when they arrived, it proved a severe disappointment. Their host, under her own roof, was a very different person from the one they had previously known as their 'beloved Coburg guest'. In her own territory 'she was one of a gay and exceedingly worldly set and we were too young to have our place among such sophisticated company.' For the two little girls whom she had promised such a wonderful time, but who were far too young to be part of the fashionable group with 'their own joys, their own mannerisms, their special language, their loves, enthusiasms and abhorrences', she now had hardly a word or a look.[5]

Moreover she had always had the ear of King Carol and Queen Elizabeth of Roumania, and as a favoured confidant of them both, they were generally too ready to listen to any unpleasant gossip or innuendo about the young British princess who in 1893 married their stolid, likeable enough but rather uninspiring nephew and heir, Crown Prince Ferdinand. Marie found it difficult to settle down at the dull court of Bucharest, and she was not always a model of discretion or fidelity. 'Cousin Charly' never thought twice about betraying any confidences.

With regard to her personal appearance, it was indeed unusual for women to have their hair so short at the time, but Charlotte's had always been unnaturally thin. At the age of seven, her mother had written of it having to be cropped down to her head as if she was a boy because of the problem.

Charlotte was also responsible for an unhelpful intervention into one particularly delicate family issue at around this time. In the summer of 1890 her sister Victoria, thwarted in her hopes to marry

Alexander of Battenberg, who had abdicated from his position as Sovereign Prince of Bulgaria, became betrothed to Prince Adolf of Schaumburg-Lippe, a match of which the Emperor wholeheartedly approved, and the marriage was scheduled to take place in November.

Yet at least two or three members of the family doubted that the wedding would ever happen. According to an exchange of correspondence between Charlotte and the Duchess of Edinburgh, even after her betrothal to Adolf, Victoria was still in love with Captain Bourke, whom she had met on board ship while they were travelling to Athens for the wedding of her younger sister Sophie to Constantine, Crown Prince of Greece in October 1889. If Charlotte and Marie were to be believed, the Empress Frederick had tried to persuade Queen Victoria to give the match her blessing. The Queen, said Marie, had been 'completely bamboozled' by her eldest daughter, had a conversation with Moretta (Victoria) and gave her a good scolding. Moretta 'took it quite lightly' and assured her grandmother that she 'never took the episode' very seriously.[6]

The Queen then gained a very different impression after talking to the Empress, who told her that Moretta 'was still madly in love with the gallant Captain', was prepared to wait for him, would have followed him to the end of the world, and was brokenhearted when Bourke broke it off. At this the Queen reportedly wept, and said that had she known it before the betrothal to Adolf, she would have helped Moretta the best she could in realising her dream. The only thing which would have frightened her was 'that dreadful tyrant Wilhelm', who 'makes rows about anything'. Queen Victoria's mind was 'in a terrible state', and she pretended that Charlotte was responsible for creating mischief. The Empress Frederick had been 'downright wicked by destroying her mother's peace of mind and happiness at the successful betrothal between Moretta and 'a real Prince'. Marie admitted that she would not have been in the least surprised if the Empress did still try and let her daughter marry Captain Bourke, and she still did not feel confident that Moretta and Adolf would become husband and wife after all.

Ever ready to pass on such stories and tittle-tattle about her family, Charlotte had given the Duchess of Edinburgh's letter to Empress Augusta Victoria to copy. The latter accordingly copied it in its entirety for the benefit of her husband, adding a letter of her own in which she said that they could never be sure of Moretta until the wedding had taken place, and suggesting that he give 'Grandmama a good talking-to', as it was surely going too far when a princess who was engaged had her own mother trying to break it off. [7]

But Charlotte was generally notorious for embellishing stories about her family, and although she had never been on good terms with the Empress, the latter was extremely strait-laced and always ready to believe the worst of any members of the family whose morals were in her opinion not above reproach. In addition Charlotte had always been on the best of terms with the Duchess of Edinburgh, an embittered woman who had never liked Queen Victoria or indeed most of her in-laws, and whose marriage to the hard-drinking Alfred had not been a happy one. If all she said was true, then that paints the Empress Frederick in a very harsh light, but otherwise one must assume that somebody was out to make mischief. After the years of unhappiness mother and daughter had suffered, largely as a result of the thwarted romance with Alexander of Battenberg, it was extremely unlikely that the Empress would have allowed her daughter to consider a marriage which would surely have been opposed just as firmly by Emperor William as the previous match had been. Some twenty years earlier Queen Victoria had allowed her fourth daughter Louise to marry a member of the Scottish aristocracy, and it is not unreasonable to assume that she would have been agreeable to one of her granddaughters forming a similar alliance with an Irish aristocrat of unimpeachable character. Yet even if she had had any influence in the matter, she and her daughter would have known at once that the Emperor would never have allowed it to happen.

As a small girl Feodora, who was largely deprived of a comfortable home life with loving parents, used to go and stay regularly with her grandmother at Friedrichshof. Charlotte had been one of eight children, and the Empress Frederick one of nine, and it was very unusual in European royal circles to be an only child. Feodora's near-contemporary, Archduchess Elizabeth, likewise the only child of the late Crown Prince Rudolf and his wife Stephanie of Austria-Hungary, was in a similar position. Elizabeth's mother would probably have liked more than one but was unable to conceive a second time for medical reasons, probably related to a venereal infection passed on to her from the Crown Prince. Feodora's nearest cousins in age were the seven children of Emperor William, and because of the antipathy between him and her mother, it was unlikely that either his sons or his daughter, who was thirteen years her junior, would ever have been playmates. It must therefore have been a lonely childhood for her, starved of parental affection and the company of contemporaries.

The Empress, who had always been particularly devoted to small children, was saddened at not being allowed to see much of the Emperor's young family, his six sons and daughter. Understandably, she was inclined to be rather sharp with them on the rare occasions when they met. The close relationship with her eldest granddaughter was some compensation. She was always very sympathetic towards her and did her best to fill the gap, and while Feodora responded warmly to her affection, her grandmother was very much concerned by what she saw as the shortcomings in her physical and mental development.

In the autumn of 1890, Feodora began to display the first symptoms of the health problems which had afflicted her mother when younger and would plague her throughout her life. She became a martyr to violent attacks of sickness, diarrhoea, shivering and pain in the head, back and limbs. About eighteen months later, when she was almost thirteen, the Empress considered her looking

> more pinched & peaky & thin than ever, with such old sharp features, much too big for her diminutive body, - and a way of talking like an old woman, she is not a bit like a child & has none of the charm & roundness of youth. [8]

A few weeks later, she was writing:

> I find dear little Feo hardly grown, she is very plain just now, especially in profile – a huge mouth & nose & chin – no cheeks, no colour – the body of a child of 5 & a head that might well belong to a grown up person! [9]

At around the same time the Empress Frederick was complaining to her daughter Victoria and to Baroness Stockmar that while Henry was becoming more amenable, Charlotte's behaviour was 'most odd', and she 'fights shy of me, hardly comes near me'.[10] Bernhard, she said, was 'impertinent' and 'ill-bred' towards her, and always ready with 'a rude and sneering remark'.[11] The behaviour of the Emperor and Empress, and of Charlotte and Bernhard, 'is a constant worry & trouble to me – but I have quite given them up, and trouble my head no more about them'.[12] Charlotte's pleasure-seeking lifestyle and Bernhard's offensive manner irritated if not offended her and indeed most other members of the family, and Charlotte's extra-marital affairs caused no end of gossip at court. About three months after Victoria was married to Prince Adolf of Schaumburg-Lippe in November 1890, her mother begged her to be 'a tender loving good & unselfish little wife!' and 'never to be to [Adolf] what Charlotte is to Bernhard!'[13]

Charlotte was also particularly close to her great-uncle Ernest, Duke of Saxe-Coburg Gotha. The elder brother, yet in many ways complete opposite, of the virtuous long-dead Albert, Prince Consort, he had long been a byword for infidelity and immoral behaviour. Since the death of Frederick III, he had sided with Bismarck in denigrating his reputation and that of the Empress Frederick, much to the disgust of the latter and Queen Victoria. The Empress was always deeply concerned when she heard that Charlotte was at Coburg, declaring herself 'always rather alarmed at all the nonsense, mischief & gossip she carries about, wh[ich] one believes, not knowing what confusion she always makes. There is a great deal of harm done in that way perhaps even unintentionally.'[14]

At one stage Charlotte decided she was going to learn Spanish. The Empress thought that nothing would come of it, as her daughter had previously made half-hearted attempts to learn Italian and Russian. Even so, she welcomed her daughter's attempts to try and achieve something constructive, as it was better 'when she has a sensible occupation to keep her at home instead of constantly having visitors & paying visits and flying about from morning to night, and leading such a foolish, aimless life, wh[ich]ends in mischief-making'.[15] Yet Charlotte proved once again that her linguistic abilities or powers of concentration were limited, and as her mother had foreseen, nothing indeed ever came of it. Before long she had returned to her 'aimless life'. 'Charlotte must go everywhere, and put herself "en evidence" – she never can keep quiet, and is always gadding about', the Empress was writing eighteen months later.[16]

She was unaware that within a few years the situation would change for the better as far as she was concerned.

One reason that Charlotte had had for consolidating her friendship with the Duchess of Edinburgh was probably the ever-deteriorating relationship with her elder brother and her subsequent need to find a new ally in the family. She still despised her sister-in-law, now Empress. Both women were very dissimilar in temperament and personality, and the breach between them was well nigh irreparable.

Early one morning in November 1892 she caused a scandal by arriving at the royal stables before an important hunt with her lady-in-waiting, Baroness Ramin. Her flushed face gave the fact away that she had 'indulged in a lively breakfast, as they say in Berlin'. Charlotte promised that she would ride *à la* Florence Dixie, the well-known advocate of women's rights, if somebody would lend her a pair of breeches. This brought forth a gentle retort from one of those present that everybody knew the princess wore the trousers in her household. After more cheery banter, she announced loudly that she would show them how 'my sweet sister-in-law', the Empress, mounted a horse. She had her animal brought round to a platform, raised herself on tiptoe, and let herself fall into the saddle with a thud 'like a majestic sack of flour', that caused the horse to stagger.

Gossip travels fast, and the next day an order was issued banning all Princesses and ladies-in-waiting from the hunt, neither Hofdamen, nor princesses of the blood royal, 'by order of the Empress'. The order, it was said, caused quite a 'sensation in polite circles'. While few people took issue with Charlotte for what she had said, they 'agreed that the Empress was right in asserting her position as vigorously as she had done'.[17]

It was only one in a long history of problems between the sisters-in-law. Within less than two years of her husband's accession to the throne, the Empress was irritating her sisters-in-law with her haughty, meddling behaviour. All of them strongly objected to being ordered about by her, and found her attitude condescending and patronising. Some thought that the Empress Frederick was inadvertently responsible for giving the Empress Augusta Victoria a sense of inferiority which made her put on airs. Yet she was always too ready to irritate people which 'rubs one up the wrong way', and Charlotte was at the forefront of those who resented her attitude.[18]

To add to the general family disharmony, the Empress's youngest sister Louise Sophie was the wife of one of the Emperor's cousins, Prince Frederick Leopold. It was common knowledge that their marriage had been an unhappy one from the start. He was widely regarded as a 'foolish, incompetent man' who treated his wife with scant consideration if not downright cruelty, while she was renowned for her bad temper and arrogance. Charlotte told her brother-in-law Ernest that she was sure Frederick Leopold was 'not quite right in his high mind & intellect, or else he is a brute'.[19] Neither of them were liked much by the rest of the family, and at one stage the Emperor's brother Henry, renowned for his easy-going manner and ability to get on well with almost everybody, even refused to speak to her because he found her attitude so insufferable.

In spite of these family feuds, relations between Charlotte and her mother remained less than harmonious. In the spring of 1891 the Empress Frederick reported to her daughter Sophie that Charlotte was planning to come and pay her a visit at Whitsuntide. She wished that she could look forward to the occasion with unmixed pleasure, 'but that I cannot, considering that she and Bernhard take the reverse view of what I do on almost every subject, and abuse me right and left behind my back.'[20]

It was sometimes almost as if Charlotte had a perverse desire to be on bad terms with and alienate so many members of her family. Even so, her differences with the Emperor and his wife would in time at least have the beneficial effect of helping to restore a more amicable footing with her mother and her other siblings.

5

'What else can one expect'
1892-1898

At around the same time Charlotte was involved, albeit tangentially, in a major scandal at court. Contrary to what some of her detractors believed at the time, she was almost certainly not the guilty party, but she was severely tainted by association, and as a result there could be no road back to general favour afterwards. A series of anonymous letters, some embellished with pornographic collages showing the faces of prominent people superimposed onto naked bodies in compromising positions, was sent to members of the court and imperial family, and neither the Emperor nor Empress were spared.

It was evident that the person or persons responsible had considerable information that could only have been known by a member or close confidant of the family. Though she had received at least one of these communications herself, with her love of intrigue Charlotte was one of the first to be suspected to be involved, if not perhaps largely responsible.

Even in the relatively restrained nineteenth-century press, where any editors who flouted censorship laws too brazenly could be arrested, such goings-on could not be kept secret. Yet further, more lurid details emerged more than a century later with the discovery of police files from the Prussian Secret State Archives in Berlin. In these it was revealed that a group of pleasure-loving aristocrats had attended a skating party and dance at Jagdschloss Grunewald, a hunting lodge in woodland to the west of Berlin, in January 1891 – at the express invitation of the Hereditary Princess of Saxe-Meiningen. They included Duke Ernst Gunther of Schleswig-Holstein, the only surviving brother of the Empress, and his mistress; Prince Frederick Charles of Hesse, who two years later would become the husband of

Charlotte's youngest and at present only unmarried sister Margaret; Baron Leberecht von Kotze, a master of ceremonies at the imperial court of Berlin; Count Frederick of Hohenau and his wife Charlotte; and a foreign ministry state secretary. The activities of some if not all, it was said by the historian Wolfgang Wippermann who had full access to all 246 letters, included much drinking, dancing and sex orgies.

The secret might have been safe had it not been for one participant, who was indiscreet enough to send the participants a series of blackmail letters from the day afterwards onwards. According to a contemporary, rather gossipy and very popular biography of the Emperor and Empress, published in 1904, the correspondent 'was in the habit of trotting out old and long-forgotten skeletons, mauling over half-healed sores, and telling of nasty or dishonourable actions, some of them true, others invented.'[1] Some of them included descriptions of what went on at the party, threatening to reveal publicly the identity of those present. Others raked up old gossip, and some included scurrilous and pornographic pictures, such as the aforementioned collages.

At first Charlotte was suspected of being behind the letters, as many of them contained gossip of which she would have had considerable knowledge. She had received letters herself, one including assertions that she had been married off quickly to Bernhard in order to avoid public scandal. It would of course have been easy for her detractors to insist that she had sent herself such missives in order to deflect suspicion, and her enemies suggested that she had hosted the party in order to trap her guests and perhaps settle old scores.

It was inevitable that word would in due course reach representatives of the court, and Emperor William himself. There was a debate in the Reichstag and in the subsequent investigation graphologists established that the letter writer was almost certainly female. The letters included plenty of gossip about the Emperor and his 'intolerable swagger' as well as his differences with his widowed mother.

Much was also said about the affairs of their sister Victoria, now Princess Adolf of Schaumburg-Lippe, who had apparently conducted indiscreet flirtations with several men at court including Baron Hugo von Reischach, a gentleman-in-waiting to the Empress Frederick, and Count Tivadar Andrássy, son of the Austro-Hungarian statesman, who had to resign his secretaryship of the Austrian Embassy in Berlin and leave Germany in order to escape her attentions. Outside the imperial family, the Duchess of Hohenau, a celebrated horse rider and wife of the openly gay Duke Frederick, was referred to in the letters as a 'randy tart'. The unflattering epithet was perhaps not undeserved, as it was common knowledge that she had sought her pleasures with high-ranking imperial servants such as Max von Baden, a future German Chancellor, and Prince Bismarck's son Herbert, a state secretary in the foreign ministry.

Others who were attacked were Alice von Schrader, the wife of a master of ceremonies and who was known to have several lesbian affairs, and the notoriously gay Prince Aribert of Anhalt, who would later be an official at the first Olympic Games in Athens. The latter was briefly the husband of the unfortunate Princess Marie Louise of Schleswig-Holstein, a granddaughter of Queen Victoria, until the marriage was annulled in 1900, leaving the princess a lonely if untroubled divorcee back in her native England for the rest of her fifty-six years.

Count Leberecht von Kotze and his wife Elizabeth were among the closest friends of Charlotte and Bernhard at around this time. They had been almost neighbours at Berlin, and their little daughter Ursula, who was the same age as Feodora, had been a regular playmate of the princess when they were small. The Count and Countess went with the Prince and Princess à quatre on an expedition to Greece and Palestine in 1892. For some reason the couples quarrelled and then went their separate ways.

At around this time Bernhard, increasingly angry with the treatment he and his wife were receiving from the Emperor and Empress, resigned from the Prussian army. He and Charlotte moved to Meiningen. Shortly afterwards the Emperor apparently relented and offered him command of the 22nd Division. Nevertheless, the brothers-in-law remained on bad terms. With regret, the Prince of Wales, who was trying for diplomatic reasons to heal the fractious relationship between himself and the Emperor, had to cancel an invitation to Charlotte and Bernhard to visit him at Sandringham in January 1894 because of the continued unpleasantness.

After tempers had cooled, in March 1895 Bernhard was appointed a general in the infantry and commanding general of the 6th Army Corps in Breslau. Husband and wife were thrilled, and for once they had good reason to be grateful to the Emperor. Charlotte wrote to Baroness Heldburg how she wished she could have witnessed 'the rushing screaming' of Bernhard and his two aides-de-camp when they received the news.

I was stunned & tears rushed to my eyes, as the telegram came: so fine in commemorating our beloved g[rand]father etc! I never before saw my husband so perfectly delighted & wild! A dream fulfilled & what a delightful future in every way! From all sides the gratulations [sic] pour in, really touching. And I!! well I feel proud of my husband, & only longed for my Father to witness our joy.[2]

According to some, it was hardly an exciting promotion, for Breslau was regarded as a sleepy, dull place, 'a city without any attractions, either social or intellectual'. The only society for them there, it was said, was of 'bureaucrats of the most starchy description, with no ideas beyond their office,' or 'impoverished landowners, belonging to the district, whose nobiliary pretensions can only be compared with the paucity of their resources, and whose conversation and even intellect is restricted to mangelwurzels, potatoes, and the different grades of fertilizers.'[3] Some might have seen the move as, in effect, only one step away from exile for him and his wife. They found the town an absolute desert after the bright lights, society and culture they had so enjoyed in Berlin. Charlotte's palace had been regarded as one of the dazzling centres of society, noted for her lively salons and good company, while Bernhard had enjoyed the company of erudite people who shared his interests, as well as ready access to his favourite libraries and museums.

Despite this, husband and wife were delighted. This was a good deal more than could be said for some of the officers at Berlin, who were annoyed at what they saw as preferential treatment by the Emperor of his brother-in-law, handing out prestigious military appointments like presents to 'minor German princelings'. Field-Marshal Alfred von Waldersee was no admirer of Bernhard, and was particularly annoyed by what he saw as unmerited promotion. These princes, he wrote in his diary, were 'without exception wretched creatures', and wherever Bernhard had served in the past, he had made himself greatly disliked because of his downright rudeness, lack of manners and inappropriate behaviour in distinguished company, his tendency to make over-hasty judgments, and 'brutal tirades against the Catholics'.[4]

Their 'exile' from Berlin may not have been solely a result of the scandal. They had lived at the Tiergarten Villa, which Emperor Frederick had rented for them on the understanding that the minister of the royal house should pay the rent as long as they lived to wish there. In the early years of his reign, when he was scrutinising the imperial accounts, Emperor William cancelled the arrangement, saying that he was no longer prepared to permit it 'not for a day, not for an hour'. Their landlord was accordingly notified that after the lease had expired in three months' time, he would no longer receive any money from the royal treasury.[5]

Neither Charlotte nor Bernhard were in a position to defy the Emperor. Bernhard had little money of his own as long as his father, still in good health, was alive. The couple were therefore dependent largely on the allowance Charlotte received as a member of the reigning house of Prussia, and therefore on the bounty and goodwill of the Emperor. He and he alone had the power to suspend any money due to them on the grounds of insubordination to his will, as well as refusing to let them leave Germany and travel abroad without his express permission, unless they went incognito and did not expect to receive the normal honours due to those of their royal rank.

On a visit to Rome in 1893 during the silver-wedding festivities of King Humbert and Queen Marguerita of Italy, Charlotte and Bernhard had been completely ignored by the Italian court, as well as by all foreign royalties present. While the German Emperor and Empress, and other invited royalties, were driving about the streets and parks in their customary royal carriages, the Hereditary Prince and Princess of Saxe-Meiningen had to make do with ordinary cabs, as they preferred to choose their own sightseeing and other diversions to pass the time. While for some modest members of royalty this may have been ideal, it was not for Charlotte, who felt insulted. Another contemporary chronicler noted that

> No one is fonder than she is of the prerogatives of rank, and like all clever and pretty women, she is ever eager to be the centre of attraction, and the object of much homage. She cannot, therefore, be said to relish the treatment and neglect to which she is subjected through her brother's displeasure.[6]

Sometimes she must have thought that the strict regime of her mother while she was growing up was to be preferred than the controlling if not vindictive sway that her elder brother was determined to exercise over her. At around this time she had planned to visit Cannes, but the Emperor forbade her to go to France, a country to which he had always taken particular exception for patriotic reasons and regarded as an enemy. Instead she had to go to Naples. The Empress Frederick was furious, writing to her daughter

Sophie in Greece that it was 'utter rubbish to order her about in that way, also to object to Cannes on account of it being in France'.[7]

Meanwhile the anonymous letters were still in circulation. When the imperial master of ceremonies, Baron Karl von Schrader, received one of these scurrilous collages, he decided that it was clearly the work of Count Kotze, who was a close friend of the Emperor but a bitter enemy of his. In June 1894 he was arrested on the orders of Schrader, who asked the investigators to search his possessions thoroughly. They examined pieces of blotting paper taken from his club and from his desk at home, and concluded that the handwriting was very similar if not identical to that of the letters.

In Kotze's defence, his friends pointed out that his father had died in a lunatic asylum, thus inferring that he was not totally responsible for his behaviour. Yet he received no sympathy at first from his old friend the Emperor, who remarked when he was told that it would cause no end of scandal that it did not matter, and he could be tried like any common criminal. He was court-martialled, pleaded his innocence and in the absence of any solid evidence was exonerated from blame. Yet he felt that he had not received an adequate official apology, and from April 1895 he fought several duels with officers who had also been at the notorious party and whom he felt had insulted him. In the first, he was wounded in the thigh. As a conciliatory gesture the Emperor presented him with an Easter egg made of decorated flowers, and several bottles of wine.

Charlotte had always been supportive of Kotze and his wife Elisabeth, and was full of sympathy for them both. To Baroness Heldburg, she wrote after the first duel how glad she was that he was 'pronounced free', but shuddered when she thought that there would have to be even more duels before the wretched affair was concluded. His wife, she said, was very courageous, behaving admirably, and her letters were 'admirable from strength of mind & will,' but the next ten months or so would prove an immense strain.[8]

At the final duel, fought a year later, he fought and wounded Baron Schrader, who died of his injuries the following day. Duelling, even to the death, was still legal in Prussia and Kotze, his honour satisfied, was given his previous post as master of ceremonies and his uniform back.

At length the letters stopped coming, and a police investigation revealed that the culprits were the Empress's reprobate brother, Duke Ernest Gunther of Schleswig-Holstein, and his French mistress, Madame la Marquise de Villemonble. Both had been friends of Charlotte and Bernhard, and it was said at the time that

Madame was responsible for 'putting the pepper and salt, the mustard and cress, into the letters'. It had long been common knowledge that the Empress's brother was no paragon of virtue, but she was embarrassed and horrified beyond measure when he was implicated. He was curtly informed that in future his time at Court at Potsdam and Berlin would be restricted to periods of one week at a time and no more, and he would not be permitted to open any establishment of his own at either place. His mistress was escorted to the German-French border under police guard, and she was warned never to show her face in Germany again.

The Emperor and Empress had unwittingly been partly responsible. It was common knowledge that the Emperor could never keep anything to himself, and his friends and adjutants kept him readily supplied with gossip which he then passed on to his wife. Although straitlaced and prudish to a fault, she was no more resistant to tittle-tattle than anybody else; she duly repeated this spicy information to her brother, who reported it back to his mistress. There were doubtless embellishments in the retelling.

Charlotte came out of the affair almost as badly. At around the time of the holiday with Count and Countess Kotze she had lost her notorious diary in which she kept her highly damaging 'secrets' about the family and court. The mistress had come into possession of this document and naturally found it invaluable as source material for her letters. During the investigation, the diary was handed to the Emperor. When he read it he was naturally furious, and he never really forgave his sister. Nobody knew for certain what happened to the diary, but another rather gossipy book of the time said that it remained in the possession of the Emperor.

Suspicion remained that Charlotte had been either the author of the letters, or else had collaborated with Ernest Gunther in writing at least some of them. She maintained steadfastly that she had had no part in such a business, and was just as innocent as Kotze, who could not 'have carried on with this nastiness systematically for 4 years, when we have travelled so much together and spent time together and often read the anonymous letters together'. The whole thing, she concluded, 'disgusts me too much.'[9] The whole business was finally laid to rest a year later, but the reputation of the court, the Emperor and his entourage, had been severely damaged. Although her morals were not perhaps completely above reproach, Charlotte was saddened and angered by what had gone on, writing in May 1895 of 'the lies, the dirt, the nastiness of which there is now documentary evidence', and that she shuddered 'to think what harm humanity can do'.[10]

Charlotte and Bernhard may have been cold-shouldered by others, but they did little to make themselves liked. Charlotte's capricious nature was not calculated to make herself popular, and Bernhard was notorious for his prejudices and reactionary opinions. He fulminated against Catholics, Social Democrats, the liberal press and the parliamentary system in general. To him the Reichstag was nothing short of a 'disgrace to German political life', 'the vilest representative body a great people has ever had in its history' and 'a collection of oxen and villains who take pleasure in keeping their nation small and powerless'. When he required additional stabling behind the general headquarters at Breslau, the Prussian Ministry of War refused to grant him permission. He was so angry that at first he threatened to 'throw everything over', until Charlotte came to the rescue by approaching a Jewish horse-dealer who offered to build them better stables for half the price. Defiantly, she wrote to Baroness Heldburg that the province would 'see the Emperor's sister helped by a kind Jew'.[11]

Relations between Charlotte and the Empress went from bad to worse. Charlotte found that Breslau had its compensations, for within a year or two she considered that she did not 'fit in' at Berlin any longer. The feud and ill-feeling between both women continued to simmer. Soon afterwards, Charlotte was complaining to Baroness Heldburg of her sister-in-law's 'arrogant condescensions', and saying that the Empress was 'disgusting, old and ugly as if she were 50'.[12] Although she was not alone in thinking that the Empress was ageing somewhat prematurely, she was only in her late thirties at the time.

In October 1896 she and Bernhard were incensed at receiving 'an insulting and impudent' letter from the Empress which made them consider withdrawing from public life altogether. The wife of their Hofmarschall, Karl-Augustus Freiherr Roeder von Diersburg, was said to have left him, and the Empress believed that it was because her husband was having an affair with Charlotte. In order to prevent any scandal from spreading, she demanded the Hofmarschall's resignation, and told Charlotte that the Emperor did not know anything about it, but 'if there was no change' she would feel obliged to inform him. Bernhard and Charlotte insisted that they were 'above such filth' and, to their credit, that they would never 'drop a faithful servant on the basis of tittle-tattle'.

Charlotte was infuriated by the Empress's 'impertinent interference' and the threat to stir her brother up against them. She was at a loss as to who had repeated such ill-founded gossip to her, 'and it proves to us once again that one can not get on with her'. Bernhard was equally enraged by the Empress's tone, and protested that she had no right to watch over everything that Charlotte did as if she was head of the family, issuing her reprimands and orders. He threatened to leave the army and retire to Meiningen as a private citizen, if it was to be their only protection against the attitude of the Emperor and Empress. This was not the first time, he complained, that she had interfered in his domestic affairs 'in the most outrageous way', and she was doing it merely to show that she had the upper hand even over German princesses who had married out of the royal house. He had a staunch ally when King Albert of Saxony offered to go and see the Empress immediately in order to make it clear to her that Charlotte no longer belonged to the house of Hohenzollern, and was thus beyond her jurisdiction.

The matter was only smoothed over when Roeder brought his wife back to Breslau and resumed his appearances in society with her by his side. Even so, Charlotte and Bernhard continued to be angry with the Empress. Soon afterwards, Charlotte decided that she was going to learn how to ride a bicycle. To the Empress, such an activity was 'indecent' for women, and she had already tried in vain to prevent her younger sister and nieces from doing so. She likewise threatened to order Charlotte to give up any such ideas, but the latter said firmly that she would not brook any interference from her.[13]

There was nothing to be done but to seek diversions elsewhere. Towards the end of 1892 Charlotte had played a discreet role in matchmaking and helped to arrange the marriage between Marie and Ferdinand, Crown Prince of Roumania, at a time when the Duke of Edinburgh and Queen Victoria were hoping that they might secure Marie's betrothal to her cousin Prince George of Wales, later King George V. Marie and Ferdinand first met at Charlotte's villa in Berlin, and they were married in Bucharest in January 1893. Now that she was cut off from the joys of Berlin, Charlotte paid regular visits to the Roumanian court, ingratiating herself with Ferdinand's uncle King Carol. During one visit in October 1895 Crown Princess Marie wrote to her mother that they were getting on particularly well with the King and Queen, and Feodora spent all day long with the Queen painting.

There was an unpleasant aspect to these visits. Jealous of the charm of Crown Princess Marie, Charlotte worked at destroying her good name in her conversations with King Carol and Queen Elizabeth. Proud of being a Hohenzollern himself, the King was disappointed that his distant kinsman had not yet paid a state visit to Bucharest. Charlotte did what she could to see it never happened, meanwhile fanning the King's resentment of Emperor William. At length her duplicitous role was discovered and she found that she was welcome no more at Bucharest than at Berlin.

Few princesses of her time had a more remarkable talent for making enemies. An anonymous observer of the day noted, all too accurately, that she had for several years 'enjoyed the just reputation in Berlin of being the most arrogant and heartless coquette at court', with her flirtations having been 'of so extravagant a character as to on several occasions give rise to unpleasant stories'. Berlin was called the 'worst place for the dissemination of scandal in all Europe'.[14] He may of course have implied it was the best, or it certainly would have been the best, for 'Charley the Brat' if she had taken more care to cover her traces.

Relations between the Saxe-Meiningens and the Empress Frederick had taken some time to thaw, if not to heal completely. Like her elder brother, Charlotte was very much a follower of the German Chancellor Bismarck, who had retired from office in 1890 after a clash with the Emperor. A year later, the Empress was writing to her third daughter Sophie, Crown Princess of the Hellenes, that Charlotte was coming to see her at Whitsuntide. She wished she could look forward to the visit 'with unmixed pleasure' but feared she could not, 'considering that she and Bernhard take the reverse of what I do on almost every subject and abuse me right and left behind my back'. In the summer of 1893, the Empress wrote to Sophie after a visit from Charlotte and Bernhard:

> It does grieve me to see her so 19th century, thinking so much of her clothes and appearances, and smoking so much. She is looking well, but her complexion is so yellow and she often smells like a walking cigar shop, which for ladies is not the thing. I shall never think it ladylike to smoke regularly and every day.

With regard to this last criticism, perhaps it was significant that one of the reasons the Duchess of Edinburgh had been disliked by the public in England was because she smoked cigarettes in public, a habit that was not considered ladylike there. The Empress did however add that Charlotte seemed pleased to be at

Friedrichshof, while Bernhard was 'very amiable and good-humoured. If they could only keep their little tongues and imaginations in order!'[15]

Charlotte was not pleased to keep her tongue in order as far as another member of the family was concerned. In her memoirs Crown Princess Marie of Roumania described an occasion in the summer of 1893, a few months after her wedding to Ferdinand when she was still a young bride and, in her words, 'only an uninteresting, ignorant schoolgirl'. Charlotte had come to the Rosenau, Coburg, for her annual visit one summer, and the family were sitting outside underneath a maple tree having tea. She and Ferdinand were in high spirits and, Marie imagined, needed 'a victim for their jokes'. They started asking her questions she could not answer, deliberately making her feel foolish. 'Nando', she knew, 'was merely being gay', but she found their teasing abhorrent. The others, even her own mother, joined in, banding together to make her feel small and ignorant, until she could take no more of it and had to run away from them. Her husband had not defended her, but had laughed with 'Charly'. It was a shameful episode which she never forgot.[16]

Throughout adolescence Feodora, who had given her grandmother such cause for concern with her plain looks and very slow physical growth, seemed hardly to improve in these respects. In January 1893, when the Empress had her granddaughter to stay at Friedrichshof, she noted that the girl's 'sharp pinched features' gave her the look of a much older person, and wished she would grow as she was still very small – 'the shortest child I ever saw'. (As the Empress and Queen Victoria were themselves both extremely short, the comment is not without significance). All the same, she was a pleasure to have around as she was so well-behaved, 'a good little child, & far easier to manage than her Mama was, - & makes one far less anxious.' Yet defects would soon creep in, and on a subsequent visit she found to her dismay that the girl was very fond of telling stories – 'and hardly ever says exactly the truth! I am afraid she will be her Mama over again.'[17]

Now an adolescent, she was taking after her mother in developing frivolous tastes. 'Her little head is always running on dress, and what people wear & look like,' the Empress wrote sadly to the Queen, aggrieved at the lack of parental guidance the child had received and feeling herself duty-bound to try and compensate. 'The atmosphere of her home is not the best for a child of her age…With Charlotte as an example, what else can one expect.'[18]

The unmaternal Charlotte was more than happy to let her daughter stay with her grandmother much of the time, so she had less need to stay at home and thus more freedom to travel abroad or enjoy society life. Feodora was prominent in the family group photographs taken at Coburg in April 1894 on the occasion of the wedding of Ernest, the young Grand Duke of Hesse and the Rhine to his cousin Victoria Melita of Edinburgh, and could be seen in the foreground of one looking up at the Empress Frederick, and in the other facing to her side with her arm on her grandmother's knee.

Later that year Feodora went on another of her regular visits to the Empress. The latter noted with regret after her departure that the young girl's parents rarely seemed to be at home, and quite often they were not even together. Her granddaughter, she lamented, 'hardly knows what home life is!' and was not surprisingly very sorry when the time came for her to have to take her leave.[19]

When Feodora was aged sixteen, the fifty-two-year-old widower Prince Peter Karageorgevich, exiled King-in-waiting of Serbia, asked for her hand in marriage. It was transparently a bid to try and strengthen his claim as heir, or at least head of the rival family, to the unsteady throne then occupied by King Alexander, but which was destined to end in bloodshed a few years later. His suit was dismissed with barely a moment's thought, and not just because of the thirty-six year age gap. Her mother declared that 'for such a throne she is far too good', and she certainly could not marry into 'such a family'.[20]

A more suitable prospective candidate for her hand then came forward. This was Prince Alfred, the only son and heir of the Duke and Duchess of Edinburgh, who had succeeded to the duchy of Saxe-Coburg Gotha on the death of the elderly and much-disliked Duke Ernest in 1893. However the young man, who was almost five years her senior, got into bad company while serving in the army, and ruined his health. The Duchess had probably been secretly hoping for her son to find himself a good wife, and maybe she held a grudge against Feodora when nothing came of it. After a visit by mother and daughter to Coburg in May 1897, she wrote to the Crown Princess of Roumania how 'Carolus' (Charlotte) 'was silent, but looked less wretched, Feo very badly dressed and not sympathique.'[21] The story would later have a tragic ending, for in February 1899 young Alfred shot himself and died of his injuries a few days afterwards.

In June 1897 Charlotte and Feodora were in England together for Queen Victoria's Diamond Jubilee celebrations. Charlotte rode in the seventh carriage of the procession with her sister Victoria, her sister-in-law Princess Irene of Hesse, and her cousin Princess Louis of Battenberg.[22]

In the first week of October Feodora was engaged to Prince Henry XXX of Reuss, a captain in the Brunswick Infantry Regiment No 92. By royal standards he was not wealthy, and he was fifteen years older than her. It was a match that the Empress Frederick would never have even dreamed of, she wrote to the Crown Princess of the Hellenes;

> It is of course not an advantageous marriage in terms of rank or position, but if Feo is happy, which she really seems to be, and the parents are satisfied, one ought to be glad. I am very glad he is older than she is, and if he is wise and steady and firm, he may do her a vast deal of good, and it may turn out very well, but she has had a strange example in her mother, and is a strange little creature.[23]

The Duchess of Saxe-Coburg Gotha, who had thought that the princess could have made a far better match, was similarly unimpressed. 'What do you say to Feo's engagement, to what seems to me, is a very bad parti?' she wrote scathingly to the Crown Princess of Roumania on 3 October. 'I never heard of that man before....How did it all come about and where are all Charlie's ambitions gone to?' The Crown Princess evidently held similar views, for she had written to her mother on the same subject that day in similar vein. 'Fancy Feo being engaged do you know this Reuss? I wonder that Charly was not more ambitious.'[24] 'This Reuss' was obviously considered a very minor German prince.

However Feodora, who had received so little affection from her parents, was evidently besotted with him. Like her mother before her, she too must have been glad to escape from an irksome home life and look forward to a life of freedom from parental constraint.

There was a partial thaw in relations between the Emperor and his eldest sister towards the end of the year. Charlotte, Bernhard and Feodora were all at Berlin to take part in his thirty-ninth birthday festivities in January 1898. From this, one must suppose that the peacemaking activities of the rest of the family had had some effect, but if so it would prove to be only temporary.

6
'This curious, loud personage'
1898-1901

The marriage of Feodora and Henry was postponed after the death of the groom's father early that same year, and this led to rumours that it had been cancelled altogether. Doubts were subsequently cast on whether it would ever take place at all. Some held the view that the general feeling in Berlin society was that the young bride-to-be had inherited 'not only much of her mother's comeliness, but likewise her fickleness, and with a girl of her particular character and temperament a long engagement is, to say the least, a mistake'.

Nevertheless the arrangements for the wedding at the end of what proved to be an engagement lasting almost one year duly went ahead. In February Feodora and her grandmother were among the guests invited to Osborne. Queen Victoria was taking a great interest in the forthcoming wedding of her great-granddaughter, the only wedding among that generation of her descendants that she would ever live to see. Like her daughter, she had become very fond of the young woman, and had a good deal of pity for her because of the difficult home life she had known.

Among the guests who arrived at Breslau in the third week of September were the princess's parents, the Empress Frederick, Prince and Princess Adolf of Schaumburg-Lippe (the Empress's second daughter Victoria and her husband), the Grand Duke and Duchess of Hesse and the Rhine, Princess Henry of Prussia, Prince Alfred of Saxe-Coburg Gotha (who had been considered as a possible husband for the bride), Duke Nicholas of Wurttemberg, King Albert of Saxony, and King William of Wurttemberg. To her regret the elderly Queen Victoria, now almost eighty, was no longer able to make such long journeys away. She was represented by her youngest surviving son Arthur, Duke of Connaught and by Sir Frank Lascelles, the British Ambassador at Berlin.

Emperor William was nearby, either attending military manoeuvres or shooting. His absence from the wedding was a somewhat tactless public reminder of the continuing family feud, not to say a public demonstration of the fact that he and the Empress had not forgiven his sister for her role in the scandal of the letters. It was commented on throughout Europe, and in contrast to the more elderly German royalties who had travelled some distance to be present.

There was speculation that he had wanted to attend after all, but the unforgiving Empress was still too angry at the role played by the bride's mother in the anonymous letters scandal to have anything to do with her sister-in-law's family. Berlin society gossips eagerly seized on this latest manifestation of ill-feeling within the family, pointing out that this snub to his sister, brother-in-law and their daughter was all the more marked as not only were all the other Hohenzollerns and several other members of the family present but various other German heads of state, who had all travelled a considerable distance. Some thought that he was even more anxious to snub his sister and her family than his wife was. To them it was obvious that the Emperor

> intended to give a public manifestation of his continued ill-will towards his sister; and that his so kind-hearted and good-natured consort should have thus joined him in this act of public discourtesy, can be explained by a story current at Berlin to the effect that she, too, feels that she can neither forget nor forgive the mingled ridicule, satire and even downright contempt expressed not only about herself, but about the emperor, her sisters, and her mother in the missing diary of Princess Charlotte.[1]

However, he gave the young couple a wedding gift of a 24-cover dinner service. Among the other gifts were a silver tea service and an Indian shawl from Queen Victoria, and a large silver jardinière from the city of Breslau.

On 23 September there was a gala performance of the opera and a large reception held by Charlotte and Bernhard, to which all the royal guests and officers at the garrison were invited.

The nuptials were solemnized on 24 September at the Lutheran Church at Breslau, by Dr von Heim, the Minister of the duchy of Saxe-Meiningen. The bride wore a gown of white satin, trimmed with myrtle and orange blossom and Venice lace, her mother's wedding veil, and her grandmother's diamond pins in her hair. After the ceremony a *déjeuner* of 180 covers was served to guests. Otherwise there was little in the way of celebrations and festivities after the wedding, and no *Fackeltanz* in the evening as there had been at that of her parents. The young couple left for Schloss Neuhoff, which was to be their home, at about 3.30 in the afternoon.

After the wedding the Empress Frederick, who probably regarded herself as more of a mother to the girl than her own mother, wrote to her daughter Sophie that she found Feodora 'very happy and quite unconcerned, not the least agitated, just as if she was going out for a walk or a drive, and in the words of a song from [Gilbert & Sullivan's] *The Mikado*, "Life was a joke that had just begun." Evidently the young people are very fond of each other.'[2]

A few weeks later it was reported by the British journal *Truth*, noted for its investigative journalism and willingness to print what other papers did not (and repeated in several other British and German newspapers), that family relations had been considerably strained by the Emperor's pointed absence from his niece's wedding. It had long been common knowledge that he was not on good terms with his sister and brother-in-law, but even so, his non-attendance had caused considerable annoyance. Queen Victoria was always keen to use what little influence she possessed with her grandson, and she had written to him asking him to make an effort to attend, 'but he was politely peremptory in his refusal, and Her Majesty does not like to have her wishes so decisively ignored by the members of her family.'[3] As one rather gossipy contemporary biographer of their German Imperial Majesties recorded, the Emperor hated family ties, was 'always at war with his mother, sometimes with Prince Henry and his sisters Charlotte and Sophie, and looks upon the rest of his relatives with supreme indifference'. As to his mother-in-law 'and Princess Feo, he loathes them'.[4]

After their honeymoon Henry, or 'Haz', was kept busy with his regimental duties. Feodora, or 'Babes', a gregarious young woman, had inherited something of her grandmother's cultured tastes, and was keenly interested in the arts. She joined a reading circle, and paid regular visits to the opera and theatre in Berlin. It was as well she had some artistic interests to keep her occupied and even fulfilled, for the family life and children for which she craved would be denied her.

Soon after their wedding Charlotte and Bernhard had bought themselves a villa at Cannes, La Forêt. This purchase had been a bone of contention between them and Emperor William. Neither he nor the Empress Augusta Victoria had any love for France, and he resented the fact that his sister should demonstrate any sense of partisanship with what he regarded as 'an enemy country' by purchasing a second residence there. Within a few years she was spending most of her winters in Cannes, and she became a familiar sight in the town as she drove around the streets in her car which she called her 'Angel'. Not only was she was much in demand among the Riviera smart set as a guest and popular as a host, but at the same time she found the Mediterranean climate vital for her health, even if neither she nor medical science were yet aware that too much sunshine was not as good for her condition as she and her doctors believed.

As a young woman she had suffered from several chronic complaints including rheumatism, swollen knees and painful joints, headaches, insomnia and a baffling blood disorder. After a consultation in August 1894 her physician, Professor Ernest Schweninger, diagnosed the trouble as 'anaemia and nervous breakdown'. It was thought that she suffered from secondary infertility. However if this had been the case, as it would have prevented a second unwanted child, this would have been the least of the worries of such a notoriously unmaternal woman. All at court were aware that she was by nature a far more dominant personality than her husband. She was also said to be less than faithful to him to the extent that she did not hesitate to take lovers, according to correspondence between Charlotte and Hermann Fürst zu Hohenlohe-Langenburg in 1884 and between the Empress Frederick and her second daughter Victoria about six years later. Nevertheless, her reputation for infidelity may have been exaggerated by gossip, and perhaps by the boasting of men at court who though that having claimed to have slept with His Majesty's sister was some kind of badge of honour.

Three portraits of Charlotte by Philip de László, who was favoured as an artist of royalty as much in his day as Franz Xaver Winterhalter and Heinrich von Angeli had been in the previous generations, date from 1899. Two of them are in private collections, one in England and one in America, and the present whereabouts of the other is unknown. All were painted early in the summer in

Silesia, and each one of them shows a woman looking somewhat tired and haggard, if not old before her time.

Taking more after her grandmother than her mother, Feodora longed to have children of her own. She was bitterly disappointed at her failure to conceive, but this was good news to Charlotte, who seemed to nurse no desire whatsoever to become a grandmother. At the beginning of 1899 Feodora was convinced that a child was on the way. In February some of the British newspapers reported that Queen Victoria would soon be a great-great-grandmother, a distinction no Queen had yet attained, as 'an accouchement' was expected that summer when Feodora's child would be born.[5] There were doubtless similar reports in the German papers as well. The would-be mother indeed wished that it could have been so, but no child ever materialised.

Feodora remained close to the Queen, who continued to keep a close interest in her, and she and Henry were guests at Windsor for several days in July 1900. Also staying there at the same time was Marie, Duchess of Saxe-Coburg Gotha, but without her husband Alfred who was seriously ill with cancer and died only a fortnight later. Unimpressed, she wrote rather scathingly to her eldest daughter in Roumania that 'Feo and her uninteresting husband are here. She looks hideous, a dried up little old fashioned chip, with hair à la madone.'[6]

As Charlotte had alienated herself from so many of her relatives, or become alienated, it would be pleasant to record that the wedding at Breslau made a difference for the better with she and Bernhard enjoying an improved relationship with their one and only child. This was clearly not the case, and whatever their initial view of their son-in-law may have been, they did not remain on good terms with him for long. In March 1899 Feodora and Henry went to stay with them, but it was not a happy time for any of them. After they had gone a very concerned Charlotte wrote to Baroness Heldburg, who was friends with mother and daughter and tried to preserve some semblance of normal family relations,

> Babes I don't find looking well, & he [Henry] grown fat heavy lumbering (& to me not sympathetic); she of course is different too, & shrinks away, whenever I try to influence her, concerning her person & health. It's of no use, so I must keep aloof & let her go her own way.[7]

Later that year she complained that her daughter was 'incomprehensible' to her. Although Feodora was 'totally wrapped up' in her husband, Charlotte thought that her daughter 'might have least have a feeling of filial gratitude for me, who did so much for her.' Feodora might well have answered with good reason that her mother had always lacked maternal feeling for her.

The Empress Frederick had always thought that Charlotte's inveterate appetite for social life, excessive smoking and perhaps drinking too much were responsible for her poor health. Recent analysis has suggested that Charlotte, her mother and her daughter, all suffered to some extent from porphyria, the non-life-threatening inherited constitutional metabolic disorder that had been incorrectly diagnosed as insanity in the case of its most famous victim, their ancestor King George III. Fellow-sufferers, it is believed, included at least three of the King's sons, namely George IV and William IV and the Duke of Kent, Queen Victoria's father, Princess Charlotte of Wales, and William IV's illegitimate eldest son George Fitzclarence, Earl of Munster. Queen Victoria may well have transmitted the gene to the Empress Frederick (but not her four younger daughters, who were apparently not afflicted), who in turn passed it to her eldest daughter, possibly her eldest son William, and her second daughter Victoria as well. A few members of the family, and political leaders in Germany and England, sometimes wondered whether Emperor William II was completely sane, and Charlotte was known to tap her forehead when friends brought up the subject of her brother's mental state in conversation.[8]

Porphyria had not yet been diagnosed, let alone understood. But Queen Victoria was subject to unexplained and seemingly illogical mood swings, and came close to what in modern terms would be regarded as a nervous breakdown after the death of her mother, the Duchess of Kent, in March 1861. After the death of the Prince Consort nine months later her immediate family, members of her household and some of her ministers, feared for her reason. She was aware of their anxiety, and at times of severe stress, would tap her head with the words, 'My reason! My reason!' As one biographer, Gerard Noel, has suggested, while her second daughter Princess Alice was nursing her during the darkest days after Prince Albert's death, 'the soundness of the Queen's mind was balanced on a needle point'.[9] Queen Victoria was more fortunate than her cousin Princess Charlotte of the Belgians, the tragic wife of the equally ill-fated Archduke Maximilian of Austria, whose short reign as

Emperor of Mexico ended in capture and death at the hands of a firing squad in 1867.

Throughout her adult life, the health of her eldest daughter also gave cause for concern. Though not subject to mood swings, her behaviour occasionally verged on the obsessive, as suggested by her attempts to marry Prince Alexander of Battenberg to her second daughter Victoria when everybody else around them were aware that it was a lost cause. As Crown Princess and thereafter, she suffered from a particular aversion to heat, which often meant that attendance at ballrooms and other social functions for a prolonged amount of time was physically impossible, and also from terrible rashes which obliged her to cover her face when appearing in public.[10]

From early childhood Charlotte, but not her younger sisters, inherited these symptoms from her mother. As a child her health had given cause for concern, and from her late thirties onwards, she was rarely well. The catalogue of increasingly severe complaints often left her irritable and unable to sleep, convinced that her 'idiotic nerves [were] giving way'. These symptoms included depression, skin complaints including severe itching, swellings, watery blisters on the skin, toothache, backache, insomnia, nausea, dizziness, constipation, acute abdominal pain, partial paralysis of the limbs and legs, and purple or red urine. Recent medical research also suggests a distinct correlation between porphyria, mood swings and stress, or severe neurotic personality disorders. The irrational behaviour of the Earl of Munster, who was thought by his doctors to be going insane and who committed suicide in 1840, was a case in point.

All this may go some way to explain the personality problems of Charlotte, who may have found some diversion or distraction from her ill-health in her love of society life and also the exceptionally bitter, long-standing feud between her and her husband with their daughter and son-in-law.

Feodora was also unfortunate enough to suffer from several of the symptoms of porphyria from girlhood, perhaps as badly as her mother, if not worse. Like her mother and grandmother, she had attacks of sickness and diarrhoea with shivering and pain in the limbs, back and head, and she would be confined to bed for several days at a time with a severe cold and migraine. It was ironic that Charlotte, whose life was blighted by similar physical symptoms if not the depression as well, seemingly lacked the empathy to understand that her daughter suffered in much the same way. With a remarkable lack of understanding, she blamed her daughter for her devotion to the life of a bright young society woman, something that she was in no position to criticise. It was a case of the pot calling the kettle black. She was similarly angry with her son-in-law for being unable to keep his wilful young wife in order.

Prince Henry, who likewise seemingly never understood the underlying physical and mental health issues which were prevalent in his wife's family, evidently resented his mother-in-law's interference and was angered by what appeared to be the passivity of his weak father-in-law. Relations between the younger and the elder generation soon went from bad to worse. By November 1899 Feodora was complaining bitterly to Baroness Heldburg about the 'disgusting' lies she claimed her mother was telling her father about her. A deeply hurt Charlotte told the Baroness that her daughter 'only causes me pain & becomes rude, I can't stand any more. The less I think of them & hear of them the better.'[1]

Following his wife's lead, Bernhard – who, some said unkindly if not perhaps inaccurately, had no mind of his own where his domineering wife was concerned – was soon writing of his daughter's 'loud mouth', and her 'mendacity and passion for gossip and calumny which she has certainly not inherited from us.'[12] A more impartial observer might have told him that she had obviously inherited it from her mother, if not her somewhat downtrodden father.

In April 1900, he declared firmly that he could not see Feodora or her husband again until she had withdrawn her accusation that her mother was a liar. After that, communication between them virtually ceased for a while. By the summer Charlotte, telling the Baroness fiercely that her daughter was 'beyond *my* comprehension', said she intended to exclude her from her home 'for ever'.[13] The issue was exacerbated by the fact that Charlotte herself was not well at the time, and also that she was gravely concerned for her mother's health.

This bitterness coincided with one of Feodora's worst bouts of ill-health to date. From September 1899 to March 1900 she had several attacks of influenza-like symptoms, accompanied by severe pain and semi-paralysis of the legs. Sometimes she was confined to bed for over a week, hardly able to move a limb except for her arms, totally dependent on her husband to lift her if she wanted to turn around. She could not even write for long, as it gave her backache. At the age of twenty-one, she must have felt like a complete invalid at least three times her age.

Once she had recovered, she went to stay again at Friedrichshof where the Empress Frederick was likewise seriously ill. After a fall from her horse in the autumn of 1898 the latter had been diagnosed with cancer of the spine. As the disease progressed she was unable to travel very far, and at length she became increasingly unable to do much for herself. Towards the end she could only go outside in a wheelchair, with the family helping her. By September 1900 she was writing – though on her worse days she frequently had to dictate her correspondence to others – that 'little Feo' was still with her; 'extraordinary little person, she reads to me a good deal, but so fast that I have difficulty in understanding it.'[14] She was concerned by her granddaughter's 'superficiality' and her physical condition, thought she was anaemic and delicate, and recommended that she ought to spend six weeks taking the cure in the Trentino. Feo and her mother were alarmed by the Empress's condition, and this doubtless had an effect on the fraught relations between them. With suffering in three generations, it was an unhappy state of affairs.

Even if she was aware of how critical her fond but frequently demanding grandmother could be, Feodora was probably grateful for her company, as it coincided with a low point in relations between mother and daughter. The Dowager Duchess of Saxe-Coburg reported to her daughter in Roumania around this time that the Hereditary Princess of Saxe-Meiningen was 'absolutely "brouillé" [fallen out] with her daughter, and 'never even hears from her'.[15]

Soon after Feodora returned home, she suffered what she called 'another attack of malaria', and took quinine which provided her with temporary relief. During the next few months she regularly complained of feeling 'rotten', and at the mercy of raging headaches which felt like hammers inside her head.

Not long after the Empress had been given her diagnosis of cancer she had confided the news to Charlotte, asking for her discretion on the subject as she did not want her enemies rejoicing in advance at the prospect of her condition and likely demise. It was a forlorn hope, and by the late summer of 1900 she was complaining to younger daughter Sophie, now Crown Princess of the Hellenes, that her illness was no longer a secret: 'I fear that she has not kept that dangerous little tongue of hers in order but has been talking about my health. It really is too bad when she swore that she would not...'[16] Yet once more she was soon forgiven. To give Charlotte the benefit of the doubt, perhaps it is fair to assume that her failure to keep the secret was not malicious, but merely because she was the kind of person unable to keep secrets. In any case, she must have been aware that before long it would be impossible for such news to be kept from the public for very much longer.

Even so Charlotte had become much closer by now to her mother, generally the most forgiving of women, and was among the regular visitors at Friedrichshof. A photograph taken of them on the terrace, probably in 1899, showed all three women posing for the camera together, with the Empress, now very ill and looking drawn, much older than her years, standing in the middle.

Charlotte continued to be at odds with the Emperor much of the time, and ever critical of the state of Germany. In the summer of 1900, he appointed Field-Marshal Waldersee as commander of the German expeditionary force in China which had been sent by the Emperor to put down unrest, following the murder in Peking of the diplomat Clemens von Ketteler. 'I do not like Waldersee's appointment! Not at all!' she wrote to Schweninger. 'That trickster, with his dishonesty, can run us straight into trouble.'[17]

Within the next few months, there were two attempted attacks on the lives of senior members of the family. Though neither had serious consequences, they came not long after an attempt on the life of the Prince of Wales in Brussels and the assassination of King Humbert of Italy in Monza. On 17 November 1900 a mentally deranged woman threw an axe at a carriage in which the Emperor and Bernhard were driving in Breslau, although neither was hit and nobody was injured.

There was a more serious incident on 6 March 1901 in Bremen, when a man, also thought to be disturbed, threw an iron buckle at the Emperor. It cut his cheek open below the right eye, leaving a wound about two inches long. Had it hit him a little higher, the results might have been far more severe. After these incidents, the court was more circumspect in announcing the travelling schedule of the Emperor, and more stringent security procedures were put into place. Charlotte was sure that neither attack had any political significance, and regarded such things as more or less inevitable from time to time, but others disagreed, thinking that increasing criticism of the Emperor in the German political parties was largely responsible for helping to foster disaffection.

In December 1900 there was another attempt at reconciliation between Charlotte and her ailing daughter. Though Charlotte must have had some sympathy for her in her constant illnesses, having long been a martyr to such symptoms herself, it did not stop her from being ready to find fault wherever she could. Feodora, she wrote, was

> pale, thin, ugly, all freshness gone, funnily dressed, hair parted
> on the forehead (like a dairy maid), talking of dancing, acting,
> Lieutenants, not looking at anything, inquiring after <u>nobody</u>!!
> I could hardly believe this curious, loud personage <u>had</u> been
> <u>my</u> Child!!...I cannot love her! & my heart seemed & felt a
> stone.[18]

Marriage to Henry, she believed, had completely corrupted her and was responsible for turning her into the shallow young woman she had become. 'How can a Child's mind be so poisoned & totally changed in 2 years by such a stupid man?' she wrote three months later. Since the wedding Henry, she said, had 'grown <u>so</u> fat, heavy and ugly', and lolled about looking '<u>so</u> done for'.[19] It was ironic that she seemed to be as ready to find fault with her daughter and son-in-law as her own mother had with her and Bernhard, and without the restraint or willingness to find extenuating circumstances that the more charitably-minded Empress Frederick had always done.

Baroness Heldburg carried on a lengthy correspondence, until 1914 in English, with mother and daughter. She still tried her hardest to act as peacemaker between them, but with limited success, for Charlotte and Feodora were becoming virtual strangers to each other. In personality they were very alike, both strong-willed characters who loved gossip and were too ready to believe the worst of each other.

It was merely a matter of time before the newly-married couple and the Saxe-Meiningens were angrily accusing each other of telling lies about them. The Empress, who was evidently dying, did what little she could to restore good relations between them, but to no avail. Any well-meant attempts at reconciliation by others, whether family or friends, simply made matters worse if anything. She was convinced that Feodora was not looking after herself properly and leading an unhealthy lifestyle. It was exactly the same criticism that the Empress had often made of Charlotte herself at a similar age.

At one stage the feud was so bitter that Charlotte not only barred her daughter and son-in-law from entering their house, declaring that the girl was 'beyond my comprehension', but also refused to allow anybody to mention their names in her hearing. Like the Empress Frederick, her other surviving son Henry and his wife Irene, who were more easy-going and far better liked than the Emperor and Charlotte, were very concerned by the state of affairs. They had always liked and felt sorry for Feodora, and they were happy to make the young couple more than welcome at their home at Hemmelmark. The amenable Henry, so often the family peacemaker, took a dim view of Charlotte's unforgiving attitude and wrote to her angrily about the way she was treating her daughter. Their relations also suffered accordingly for some time as a result.

Feodora's visit to Windsor in the summer of 1900 was the last time she ever saw her great-grandmother. Anxiety over the Boer war, and the loss of her second son Alfred, Duke of Saxe-Coburg in July and her grandson Prince Christian Victor of Schleswig-Holstein three months later, all undermined her health. By the time she and the court reached Osborne just before Christmas, it was clear to her physician and at least some of her family that she was unlikely to live much longer. A procession of children and grandchildren, the Emperor William among them, gathered around her bedside as she was sinking and died on 22 January 1901.

According to reports in *The Times*, Henry of Reuss was among relations who were present at the Queen's funeral at Windsor in February 1901, but his wife was not. As Feodora had been so devoted to her great-grandmother, it was probable that ill-health prevented her from joining him.

Much as she had desperately wanted to return to England one last time, the ailing Empress Frederick was also unable to attend the final obsequies of her mother. Some of her last letters to Queen Victoria, written when she was bedridden and slowly dying from cancer, too weak to hold a pen or pencil, were in the handwriting of Charlotte, who took turns in keeping vigil by the bedside. She and her sisters were regular visitors to Friedrichshof during their mother's declining months as she was wracked with pain, often screaming in agony, and they devoted much of their time to looking after her. Perhaps their shared physical suffering, albeit from different causes, had brought mother and daughter together again properly – and just before it was too late. All six of the Empress's children were at Friedrichshof when she finally found release, aged sixty, late on the afternoon on 5 August 1901.

7

'Like a small erupting volcano'
1901-1914

About a year after the Empress Frederick's death, Charlotte and Bernhard had heard, or at least told Baroness Heldburg, that they believed Feodora had been telling 'fearful lies' in order to try and get money out of her grandmother during her last months. The Empress had never been particularly wealthy, but she was always kind-hearted and generous to a fault to family and friends. The granddaughter who had virtually regarded her as her own mother instead of Charlotte, and found in her a more understanding and congenial personality, may have found her a soft touch. Yet as Charlotte and Bernhard were always ready to believe the worst of their daughter, their assertions have to be regarded with caution. Mother and daughter were evidently as bad as each other with their propensity for lying and mischief-making. That their chronic physical ailments almost certainly had some impact on their mental health as well merely exacerbated an already difficult situation.

While Feodora apparently believed, or told others, that her illness was a virulent form of malaria, Charlotte thought that the doctor's diagnosis was concealing something far more sinister. She refused to believe such an innocent explanation, and instead she told her brothers and sister Victoria, apparently without any evidence whatsoever, that her daughter had contracted venereal disease from her husband. To the Baroness, she wrote that she could not entrust to pen and paper the name of her condition, but there was absolutely nothing to be done, except for the young couple to submit themselves to a long course of treatment which both of them flatly refused to undergo.

Feodora was equally outraged by her mother's claims. demanded that her daughter should have the opportunity to prove her case by allowing herself to be examined by Professor Schweninger, and took her outright refusal to do so as an admission of guilt. Feodora and Henry informed several members of the family, among them the Empress and the Emperor's brother Henry, of Charlotte's 'incredible' behaviour. They agreed that the latter had been very high-handed, and advised the couple that they should certainly not set foot in her mother's house until she had withdrawn her accusations.

Various other members of the family were keen to try and reconcile the warring elements. In February 1903 Charlotte and Bernhard celebrated their silver wedding, and Henry and Irene laid on a celebration for them at the castle at Kiel. Prince and Princess Adolf of Schaumburg-Lippe were invited, as was Feodora – though in Princess Adolf's pleasantly-written if somewhat bland memoirs published in 1929, there is no reference to her husband Henry being one of the gathering. It included a luncheon party on Henry's ship, and in the evening a visit to the theatre to see a performance of *Die Zärtlichen Verwandten* ('The Affectionate Relations'). Again, according to the memoirs, the princess thought it amusing that the play should consist of the family members quarrelling among themselves, 'whereas we were really a most harmonious family'.[1] As was so often the case, she was in denial. Bearing in mind her and her siblings' problems with her eldest brother and his wife, harmonious was rather too kind a word.

As much of the former Princess Victoria of Prussia's book makes clear, she was never one to reopen old wounds or advertise family differences. Subsequent history suggests that a truce may have been called out of respect for Henry and Irene, but in reality nothing had really changed. If Feodora ever read her aunt's memoirs, she could be forgiven a wry smile at reading the statement that Charlotte and Bernhard 'had one daughter who was the apple of her parents' eye'.[2]

It may hardly be necessary to add that the references to Charlotte in her younger sister's memoirs, few though they may be, are always generous and affectionate. After going into exile in Holland the former Emperor William wrote a personal memoir, *My Early Life*, published in 1926, but any mentions of his eldest sister (and in fact all his sisters) in the text are very brief and perfunctory.

Charlotte's health was still often unsatisfactory, and she was spending more and more time at Cannes, particularly in the winter and spring. In the summer of 1903, she reported to Dr Schweninger that her nerves were 'in shreds, although my appearance does not show it. But a terrible headache on one side & dizziness on the left side *so* depress me, & completely irregular feelings of malaise, with a rash & itching'. At the same time, she complained that she had been suffering for several weeks from neuralgia over the left eye, and from severe vomiting.[3]

Three years later, she reported swollen joints and acute pain, alternately in the back, arms and legs, as well as 'moaning, wailing, poor appearance, even worse mood & constipation'. The doctors tried to persuade her it was gout or rheumatism, but she thought it was more likely to be influenza, of which there was an epidemic on the Riviera at the time.[4] Within a week, she was having to take aspirin as she could no longer bear the 'excruciating pain' in her eye sockets, nose and forehead. For the first time, she reported that her urine was dark red, later identified as a positive symptom of porphyria. The other symptoms included sciatica, rheumatic pains and dental abscesses, afflictions that had been endured by her grandfather the Prince Consort in the last few weeks of his life. She was often confined to bed as she was too ill to get up and enjoy a normal life. As the condition was as yet undiagnosed, some of her doctors considered her ailments hysterical in origin.[5] It is hard to believe that she did not recognise similar problems with her daughter's health.

Seven months later, in November 1906, she wrote again to Schweninger of her symptoms, but at the same time waxed lyrical about the atmosphere at Cannes, so different from inhospitable Berlin; he should, she told him, 'come and see this wonderful, sunny land; one simply cannot but recuperate both in body and soul here'. Thirteen days of torture, she went on, had quite 'drained' her, and she was spending most of her time either lying down or sitting outdoors as she asked his advice for any way of alleviating the swelling and itching; 'The rash on my upper body is enough to drive me mad!'[6] Her condition only deteriorated during the next few weeks. A month later she told him she had been confined to bed for five days with dizziness and fainting spells, only seeing stars against a black background, and plagued with rash, itching and abdominal pains.[7] Three weeks later, various remedies she had tried were doing nothing for her; the dizziness and itching were getting worse, and she was 'constantly nauseous'.[8]

Schweninger brought his assistant, the psychoanalyst Georg Groddeck, to Cannes several times so he could examine her. In the spring of 1907 she visited his clinic in Baden for the first time. His treatment initially provided some relief. When he treated 'the bad patches' in April, it was 'quite excruciating', but he hoped that massage twice daily and hot compresses each morning and evening would effect a cure within two or three weeks, a treatment which she likened to 'being flayed'.[9]

Six months after this, she could report that the massage had indeed been effective for a while. She spoke too soon, for only a few days later she was begging for morphine drops to alleviate the old pains, which had returned with full force. They were accompanied by intense nausea which had her close to fainting, with a burning, stabbing pain extending into the left side of her abdomen, and itching which had flared up all over her body.[10] Over the next few months her letters continued in similar vein, as she reported the same persistent symptoms of pain, constipation, dizziness, nausea, cramps, abscesses, itching and altogether absolute torture, with only occasional relief and sleep from morphine.

At the end of 1903 Henry was transferred to Flensburg, close to the German-Danish border, in a region renowned for its mild climate. It was also close to Hemmelmark, Kiel, the home of Feodora's uncle Henry and aunt Irene, with whom Feodora had always got on well. They found a small house with a garden that she found a pleasant diversion to occupy her time. She began to put on weight, took long walks and for several months she felt much stronger than she had for a long while. Later she bought a horse so she and her husband Henry could go on early morning rides together.

Yet she was still upset by the lingering feud with her parents, anxious about the state of their finances (suggesting that they might have relied a little too much on the generosity of the Empress Frederick), and her persistent failure to become pregnant never ceased to trouble and frustrate her. After four weeks spent at a sanatorium at Langenschwalbach, run by Dr Frank, the brother of Baroness Heldburg, she fervently hoped she would be able to conceive at last. But the treatment proved a total failure, as she wrote in despair that the cure had 'turned my inside topsey turvey', and that 'these everlasting disappointments are too disgusting'.[11] When Charlotte had been told three months earlier that there was a possibility she might become a grandmother, she retorted angrily, 'No thanks, I can live without the damned brood!'[12] It is tempting to wonder whether she might have commented more charitably if she had not been in almost perpetual pain herself. On the other hand, she might have foreseen that in view of the health problems of her daughter and herself, and grandchild would almost certainly be a similarly sickly infant.

Henry thought the best thing for his ailing wife would be to go to a spa on account of her anaemia. His personal view was that spas would not really do her condition any good, and 'things like that usually pass with time', but at least it might lift her spirits. She had recently been prescribed arsenic and thorium pills and put on weight while she was taking them, but as soon as she stopped doing so she reverted just as quickly to her usual thin and pale self.

However the periods of ill-health were never far away. Regular bouts of toothache and migraine continued to plague her, and another bad bout of what she suspected was influenza in October left her listless for a long time afterwards.

In spite of this, she never ceased in her determination to try and have a child, no matter what she might have to go through first. She went to a couple of private clinics in turn. The first was one run by Reinhold Franz, and after she was dissatisfied with this one she attended another in the Sonnenstrasse, Munich, where she was under the care of Professor Albert Döderlein, director of the Department of Gynaecology at Munich University. Though it was painful, she told the Baroness in July 1909, 'the more I suffered, the happier I was, as it was for Haz, for his future happiness, I should gladly have borne more, & the greater the pains, the surer I felt, that Döderlein was getting at the root of all evil, & I nearer my prize.'[13]

When she was discharged, and went back to Brunswick where they had now made their home, Döderlein urged her that she needed to make an effort to avoid all 'malarial areas' and must not travel anywhere by train. He also encouraged her to walk and drive as much as possible. Her chances of conceiving should now be good, he said, but she should return to Munich if she was not expecting within the next three months.

Sadly for her she was not, and by January 1910 she was once again a patient at the clinic. She was also trying to cure the pain and lameness from which she had suffered since her severe attack of influenza in the winter of 1907-8. The professor warned her that it would not be possible for him to alleviate her pains and complaints unless he was allowed to subject her to a course of treatment which would take several weeks at least. In order to undergo this, she would have to remain in the clinic until he had solved the problem, and she would then have to keep away from all excitement for at least three more months. Despite his diagnosis, and despite her suffering from 'terrible, dreadful colic and fainting fits', in February

1910 he went ahead with an attempt to inseminate her artificially. It was a delicate operation which came close to costing her her life.

Feodora told her aunt Katharina that for three days afterwards she had been at death's door, although the aunt suspected she was exaggerating the severity of her condition in order to crave sympathy. Yet she did not blame Döderlein at all, whom she called 'so safe & great as Operateur'. She admitted that he had made a mistake, but she was never angry with him for a moment or even doubted him, believing that he was doing the best for her that he could; 'a Professor is human, & mistakes are human too.'[14]

After a second operation in September 1911 left her even weaker than before her husband, the professor, the Baroness and at last Feodora herself begged her parents to come and visit her. Charlotte wrote to her for the first time in almost a decade, expressing bewilderment at her condition and outrage that what she regarded as an unnecessary and unwise operation should have been decided on; 'those murderous knives are too wicked & dangerous.' She warned that such a procedure could very well prove fatal, and could not see what purpose such an operation might serve. 'You were ever a strong & healthy girl & all your internal organs were in perfect condition & order; so what has suddenly made yr. inside go so wrong, I fail to comprehend or take in.'[15]

Once again she came to see her listless and still sick daughter the following year, after the latter was discharged from the sanatorium. This time she put the blame on patient and professor equally, calling her daughter a lost cause; 'Slightest exertion finishes her out, always layed [sic] up. Can't do anything as she won't listen; hopeless case.'[16]

In the wake of the anonymous letters scandal, relations between Charlotte and the Emperor had never improved. She frequently despaired of the Emperor, and after one particularly high-handed comment of his on the Prussian landed aristocracy in 1901 she had written to Dr Schweninger in expressions redolent of her mother, 'Après nous le deluge, God knows! One cannot but be deeply sad and serious, facing the future with open eyes!'[17] Two years later, the Social Democrats in the Reichstag shocked the Emperor, his chancellor and the government when they increased their representation in the Reichstag at the expense of the German Conservatives. Charlotte wrote sarcastically that the elections were 'just wonderful' as they 'suit our decadence, more and more covered up with speeches and festivities!'[18]

Further elections to be held in January 1907 also alarmed Charlotte, with the possibility of the Conservative and Liberal parties both loyal to the Reich losing votes to the left-wing Social Democrats and the Centre, who would probably combine to form a pact if they attracted enough votes between them. She doubted that a new election would bring any improvement to the unsettled situation. 'We are not prepared for the onslaught, and Bülow least of all!!' she wrote in alarm to Schweninger. 'The future looks very very dark to me.'[19] In the end the worst fears of the Emperor, his sister and his chancellor were not realised. After the Social Democrats lost about half of their seats, she could write with relief that Bülow was triumphant and that they were 'holding on to him' more firmly than ever before.

But she was not the only one to believe that the future looked bleak. A scandal, which threatened to dwarf that of the anonymous letters and pornographic collages affair of the previous decade, had long been simmering beneath the surface. The journalist Maximilian Harden, journalist, editor and publisher of *Die Zukunft* ('The future'), a weekly radical journal sympathetic to the cause of social democracy in Germany, claimed to have evidence of homosexual conduct between prominent members of Emperor William's entourage, notably Philipp, Prince of Eulenburg-Hertefeld, and General Kuno von Moltke. Accusations and counter-accusations multiplied, Harden exposed both men as practising homosexuals, and in the process further senior ministers and others close to the entourage of the Emperor and Crown Prince were also implicated and accused. From 1907 onwards there were several cases of criminal libel brought before the court. Harden assumed that the accusations were common knowledge throughout Germany, but in the process it emerged that the Emperor had been shielded from much, if not all, of the gossip and scandal. His absolute horror at learning of the extent of homosexuality and the involvement of several of his circle can be imagined.

The more worldly Charlotte, who had moved in different circles and was much better informed than her brother, had long been aware of the facts. She followed Harden's campaigns approvingly and gave him her support. She considered that his revelations were 'masterly', although his disclosures might be distressing for some in high places. To some she seemed to take a perverse pride in being his only champion as far as her family were concerned, as the rest of them condemned him as a 'vile scoundrel, insolent Jew, brute etc.'[20] To her it was obvious that anti-Semitism prevailed, and that there was a deliberate attempt to hush up the matter, and she deprecated the 'blindness, mawkish sentiment, apathy, stupidity, false sympathy with H.M.'[21] to which everybody else subscribed. Everybody else, she thought, was complicit in trying to suppress the truth, which was bound to come out sooner or later; and she was more farsighted than them in realising that the longer her brother and those closest to him tried to contain the matter, the worse would be the damage to imperial Germany and in particular the imperial family when the sordid details did eventually emerge.

In February 1907 she was aghast when the public prosecutor's office maintained that the prosecution of Harden for libel was not in the public interest, and she urged Moltke to bring a private prosecution against him for libel instead. 'Have these people gone mad?' she wrote to Schweninger. 'Do they really want to dispute this? The whole world knows about it.'[22]   It was almost as if the whole world except the Emperor and select members of court knew all or at least some of the facts. As she feared, it was a squalid business from which neither the crusading Harden nor the hypocritical court and imperial establishment would emerge with credit and without damage.

To the Emperor's horror, at one stage there was every possibility that Charlotte and Bernhard might be summoned as witnesses in one or more of the trials, and he dreaded the names of friends and family being 'dragged through the dirt of all the gutters of Europe' for all the journalists to report on in detail. In the end this never came to pass, and the disgraced Eulenburg escaped justice only because his trial was repeatedly postponed and finally abandoned on the grounds of ill-health. Given Charlotte's own ever-worsening condition, health might have been an adequate reason for excusing her from having to appear in court as well.

Domestic imperial matters took a turn for the worse the following year, and Charlotte was very angry when moved to make what was for her a rare public comment on current affairs in the autumn of 1908. The Emperor had made himself look foolish with his so-called 'interview' with Colonel Edward Stuart-Wortley, a friend who had written up a series of relaxed but rather indiscreet conversations they had had together while he was staying on holiday in England the previous year. They were subsequently published with minor alterations – and without ministerial vetting - that October in the *Daily Telegraph* in London. This proved to be the worst crisis of his reign prior to the outbreak of the First World War. Reaction in Germany and Britain was quite the opposite to what he had intended, and his self-confidence so severely shaken as a result that at one point he took to his bed, telling his family that he intended to abdicate.

His sister then twisted the knife in the wound. She remarked publicly that the only salvation for Germany and Europe would be the formation of a collective regency of all the German princes, under the aegis of somebody generally respected by all. The obvious choice, everyone believed, would be the much-liked and admired Prince Ludwig, at the time Regent of Bavaria on behalf of his deranged nephew King Otto and later King Ludwig III. Such a move would probably be enough to restrain any more of the Emperor's 'initiatives' in future.

To Professor Schweninger, she expressed herself bluntly about what she called the shameful state of German affairs. Insisting that her brother had got himself into an impossible situation, and that she was the only one who was making any effort to try and help him, she said that she would like to persuade the German Princes to go to the Emperor unanimously if possible, 'putting their silly individual rights aside for once, and offer him their help in the name of the Reich and in the name of their peoples, under clearly-stated conditions'. This, she was sure, was the only thing that had any chance of making a suitable impression on him. All she sincerely wanted was to try and help her brother, and she was sure that Bülow, the imperial chancellor, and his cronies, were the Emperor's undoing. She was convinced that they had been far more to blame than their imperial master, who 'thinks himself infallible', and she was 'deeply pessimistic about the future of our German political, dynastic and governmental affairs'. The Bundesrat, she said, was 'a comedy, the Ministers likewise, we are left standing alone, sunk in the deepest mire, and as a loyal Prussian I am ashamed.' Her husband, she alleged, was inclined to laugh at her and her efforts to try and ameliorate the situation, and said he was sure that she would never be able to persuade the gentlemen to do such a thing. If this was the case, she believed, then they were not fit to remain as ruling princes.[23]

Her initiative was never pursued, and she never felt inclined or indeed able to take it any further. Yet had she done so, it is unlikely that the Emperor would have received her well-intentioned ideas kindly or taken her at all seriously.

Meanwhile, her health remained as poor as ever. Much as she enjoyed being in Cannes and having the benefit of more temperate weather, it only seemed at this stage to be starting to dawn on her that winter holidays in sunshine were merely exacerbating her agony. The time had not yet arrived when it was established that sun was something that sufferers from porphyria needed to avoid at all costs. Over Christmas 1908 and the new year she was often unable to get up and out of bed because of the pain, and only hot water bottles offered any relief. In addition to the previous symptoms she had also developed ulcers in her mouth, nose and on her behind, and she felt 'like a small erupting volcano'.[24] Her condition, she wrote, was altogether 'unbearable & takes away the last remaining bit of joie de vivre'.[25]

The constant catalogue of Charlotte's miseries and physical suffering, relayed in all its medical detail in letters to Dr Schweninger, makes dispiriting reading. To add to her existing woes, by early November 1909 she also had raging pain in her teeth and nerves which lasted several days. One night, she recorded, she 'screamed and ranted for five hours,' and at 3 a.m. an assistant had to be summoned to give her an injection which took an hour to alleviate the agony. Her head, teeth, and 'every inch' of her mouth, as well as her hips were afflicted with the pain. At around noon the attacks abated, but by that time she was completely exhausted from her 'ranting and raving' during the night when she woke everybody up.[26]

In spite of this she still found the strength to make the journey to England just over eighteen months later. In June 1911 she was among the family guests who converged on London and attended the coronation of her cousin King George V, and she stayed in the country for several weeks afterwards. One can but hope that by this time she was on better terms with the new King's consort Queen Mary, who on one occasion when asked which of her cousins she disliked the most, allegedly chose 'Charley the Brat'.

While she was staying at Sandringham with her English cousins in July, Charlotte wrote enthusiastically to Baroness von Heldburg that 'What I've seen, learnt to admire, heard & witnessed, I can't describe. There is no place in the world like England, & if possible I'm more English than ever.' While she was there she made several expeditions, usually with her brother Henry, with whom she was now on the best of terms, to hospitals, 'various lovely country houses', and 'marvellous private collections'.[27] One of these dwellings was Badminton House, Gloucestershire, where she and her sister-in-law Princess Henry were on the jury of ladies taking part in awarding prizes to the best cars in the English and German teams for the 'Prince Henry tour', an Anglo-German car rally which had started in Hamburg early in July and finished in London almost three weeks later.[28]

The Empress Frederick would have been reassured to know that in later life her eldest daughter had become quite Anglophile in her sentiments, and often waxed lyrical about England. In fact Charlotte was becoming more and more like her mother had become in widowhood. Both were alternately in despair and angry at the direction of German affairs under Emperor William and his ministers, and frustrated in their inability to do anything about it but vent their indignation in correspondence to their closest confidants.

Not surprisingly the heat of the English summer soon had an adverse effect on her health. Not long after her arrival her joints, feet, hands and eyes swelled up to an intolerable extent. She wrote to Schweninger that at one point she was forced to take to her bed for several days with excruciating pains and a face swollen beyond recognition, leaving her unable to speak or even eat because of swollen tonsils, glands and gums.[29]

When the Emperor was also suffering at around this time from oedema, swellings on his neck and forehead and other irritations, she thought that he must be suffering from the same disease as she was. To Schweninger, she wrote in 1912 that he was neglecting his health, not looking after himself properly, and treating his oedema in 'a stupid and completely mistaken' fashion.[30]

Relations between the increasingly pain-ridden Charlotte and her elder brother, which had since passed the point of no return, deteriorated even further in November 1912 when the German General Staff considered that mobilisation against other European powers would be a possibility before long. They evidently felt that a clearing from the ranks of some of the personnel who were past their best on grounds of age was in order. Bernhard was one of several older army officers who found themselves pensioned off from the army without notice. He had reached the age of sixty-one, but this did not reconcile him or Charlotte to the decision. She was outraged on behalf of her husband at such treatment, complaining bitterly that he had received his dismissal, 'coldly & curtly', and that 'H.M. has no further use for him whatever...I shall try to keep my outrage to myself'.[31]

In between her spells of what verged on debilitating ill-health, Feodora also visited England from time to time. In September 1913 she was invited to stay at Croydon Hall, Somerset, a grand country house on Exmoor owned by Count Conrad von Hochberg, an

Anglophile distant cousin of the Emperor who had blood ties to the Reuss family. While she was there she paid a private visit to Exeter, where she was welcomed by the Mayor and the deputy town clerk, who showed her ancient charters, seals and regalia at the Guildhall, in an exhibition in the Mayor's parlour. She also spent some time in the cathedral, where members of the chapter pointed out several objects of interest to her.

Sadly there would be no more sojourns for her in England after this for a good many years. Within less than a year, both nations would be at war.

8

'Now on a throne'
1914-1916

O n 25 June 1914 Bernhard succeeded his father George as Duke of Saxe-Meiningen. Aged eighty-eight, the late Duke had long suffered from deafness and retired from public life, devoting himself to his antiques and collection of manuscripts.

A few weeks later an article appeared in the *New York Times*, headed 'The Kaiser's Cleverest Sister Is Now On a Throne'. It had been written by the diplomat who had accompanied them to Paris shortly after their marriage, and who noted that in spite of the Emperor's intense dislike of their European neighbour, they had recently been able to spend a certain amount of time openly in France. The writer observed that she had always been famed for her 'independence of character', and that during that expedition she and her brother had both revelled 'in their emancipation from the parental apron strings', although perhaps he meant 'fraternal'.

This independence, it was observed, was bound to lead to later friction with her brother after his accession to the imperial throne as he always demanded total submission to his authority. It was something the sharp-tongued princess would find beyond her. Their relations would also be strained by the Emperor's belief that she 'was setting his authority at nought, that she was encouraging rebellion in Berlin society, of which she was the acknowledged leader, and even among members of the royal family'. Her witty stories were twisted when presented to the Emperor by those who wished to strain relations between them, and had been partly responsible for the departure of Charlotte and Bernhard from Berlin. Charlotte, he concluded, was 'a law unto herself' and the 'most brilliant, gifted, and fascinating' of the Emperor's sisters.[1]

Mention was also made of the cleverness and intellectual prowess of Bernhard, who was described as a man of 'great culture and erudition' who possessed a 'remarkable knowledge of modern and ancient Greece'. This had enabled him travel widely throughout the country of his brother-in-law King Constantine, and to write several dramas in modern Greek which were produced successfully in Athens.

However, this pleasant existence was about to come to an end. Three days after Bernhard's accession came the assassination at Sarajevo of the Austrian heir Archduke Francis Ferdinand and his wife Sophie at Sarajevo. On 4 August, Britain and Germany declared war, and Bernhard had to put aside his scholarly interests and pursuits as he left for the front.

Charlotte was therefore nominally in charge of the duchy, but she had no need to be any more than a figurehead, as government was in the hands of others. It was just as well, for physically and mentally she was ill-equipped to take any part in administration of the state. At length Bernhard was obliged to return and resume his role.

By the winter of 1917-8 she was complaining of regular kidney pains, digestive and internal disorders, constipation, toothache, boils and oedema. The skin on her face had become wrinkled, peeling and itched badly. Any kind of activity was a major effort, restricted largely to hobbling around her room on two sticks for short periods. With the lack of exercise, her feet and legs had become atrophied and very thin.[2]

Shortly after the outbreak of hostilities in August 1914, her son-in-law Henry went to serve on the western front. By this time he was losing patience with his wife, her chronic ill-health and what he called her 'operation mania'. He refused to give his consent to an operation which he was sure would be 'worse than useless'. After talks with Dr Haedke, who had taken her on as a patient the previous year, he was convinced that she was a lazy good-for-nothing who would rather be in hospital where she was cared for better than she could ever be at home. She had readmitted herself solely for her amusement, he thought, and because she could not be bothered to look after herself. Many upper-class German women, he maintained, were unable to cope with the loneliness after their husbands had left to fight and were spending their days in bed. What, he asked, if men were to do the same? Her illness, he believed, 'consists mainly in complete lack of energy and mental apathy'.

When he visited her in the mornings he found her cheerful enough, smoking, eating and laughing with the nurses. If he asked her how her night had been, she would put on a miserable face, say that she had not slept at all and had had a high temperature, all of which existed only in her imagination.[3]

She did her duty to her empire as a good German by opening a small hospital for wounded soldiers, but he unkindly dismissed her efforts as 'a farce'. Soon she was back to the old cycle of headaches, depression, lameness, mental debility, and another visit to the clinic of Professor Döderlein, which did nothing to make her feel any better. Henry complained that her heart was perfectly normal, and the symptoms only reappeared every time she was supposed to do something that did not suit her. She grossly exaggerated her illnesses, causing him and others quite unnecessary anxiety.[4]

Nevertheless he consented reluctantly to her undergoing another operation in February 1916, after she had been suffering from severe pains and vomiting. The result seemed to bear out the opinion of her husband and her mother (who until then were not normally noted for agreeing on anything) as well as others who had regarded it as quite unnecessary. Her appendix was discovered to be so insignificantly affected, and the pains of which she had complained were not commensurate with the medical findings. She was due to leave hospital in early March, but Henry for one was sure that it would not be the end of the story. He had 'stopped measuring anything by the yardstick of normality'[5] and was prepared to let matters take their course, as he recognised that he no longer had any influence whatsoever over her or the patience to advise her. By now he was demanding that she should enter a sanatorium for the rest of the war, where she would have a doctor to look after her and some company for mental stimulation, but his demands were ignored.

In March she was suffering severe pain once more, including an inflammation of the nerves in the back and the ribs. Sometimes she was unable to move and all she could do was to cry out loud. At one stage she was also having heart cramps, two or three times a day. Her parents came to visit her, but it was not an agreeable experience for any of them. Afterwards she wrote to Baroness Heldburg that while her mother Charlotte was there she had behaved 'absolutely unbelievably'. For some reason – perhaps because she was in pain herself - she utterly refused to visit the wounded or to distribute any of her signed photographs in the hospital, thereby causing great offence and resentment among soldiers and staff. After her parents were gone, Feodora suffered terrible cramps once more.

By May she was discharged from hospital and sent home again. She insisted that she had recovered and for a short time appeared to be her old self. However, before long she was back to the old pattern of alternating between elation and abject misery. Henry found her mood swings, ecstatic one moment and 'depressed unto death' the next, hard to bear, and very difficult to live with. Any lingering suspicions that she was malingering were apparently confirmed, he thought, when he joined her in June 1916 while he was on leave. For some days she appeared in the best of health and spirits, full of energy; 'she clambered about the mountains with me for hours, has a wonderful appetite and sleeps well; not the slightest sign of heart or nerves.'[6]

A similar break with Baroness Heldburg and her husband at their chalet in the Bavarian Alps a month later had them and Henry all close to despair. During this time Feodora was not only in rude health but even behaving, as they saw it, quite recklessly. One has to conclude that the regular routine of fresh air and proper walks did her good, and the less time she had to sit around moping or fretting about her ailments the better it was for her. Although she clearly suffered much, her husband had lost patience with her perpetual complaining about her ailments, and felt she would do well to bear with them the best she could. When she returned to Neuhoff she had changed markedly for the worse and was ill once more, complaining about an internal chill that left her with pain and a high fever.

Sometime around Christmas 1916, it appears that Feodora and the Baroness fell out with each other. The younger woman, it is supposed, had said, written or done something to offend the woman who had been more or less like a mother to her for over twenty years, and if so she was probably too stubborn to apologise.[7] Their friendship and correspondence then abruptly ceased.

In a later, more sympathetic age, Feodora would almost certainly have been diagnosed with manic depression or bipolar disorder. Such a condition had not been properly recognised until the later years of the nineteenth century by the German psychiatrist Emil Kraepelin. The age had yet to come when depressives were treated with understanding instead of contempt, and it is probable that Henry never considered the possibility that a daughter and wife had a genuine mental health issue which needed careful handling instead of total denial. As Charlotte probably suffered from depression as well as many of the chronic ailments with which her daughter was afflicted, one can only wonder why she treated her with such a lack of understanding as well.

But by this time, Charlotte was by now too wrapped up in her own health problems to consider those of her unloved daughter. She was increasingly racked by pain with swollen legs and feet, kidney problems, intestinal disorders and chronic aches throughout her body. Regular visits to the sanatorium and almost perpetual medical supervision brought her no relief.

One of her family therefore had good reason to be grateful for her solicitude at a time of sadness. In July 1916 her brother-in-law Prince Adolf of Schaumburg-Lippe died after a short illness. Early in their married life Victoria had had a miscarriage, and never had the children she and her husband had so dearly wanted. After he passed away she was very lonely. Although the sisters had never been particularly close, Charlotte made a special effort to be beside her at this time. 'To her I was always the young sister who had to be petted,' Victoria later recalled. 'She was so kind and good to me, and the visits that I paid to her were full of joy and interest.'[8] She would always remember how her ailing elder sister Charlotte was such a comfort to her in the first sad weeks of her bereavement.

9

'In great pain'
1917-1945

During the war Charlotte's health, which had never been very robust, continued to become progressively worse. She had attempted all possible remedies, but apart from morphia to alleviate the pain, there seemed to be no suitable treatment or cure for the recurring symptoms which caused her so much suffering. Schweninger's assistant George Groddeck, in whose clinic she was spending a good deal of time, could do little more than try and make her as comfortable as possible. By December 1917 she was almost unable to walk, and could do little more than hobble around on sticks in her room for short periods at a time. Eleven months later, when the end of the war in brought the final curtain down on the German empire and all her duchies, she was increasingly weak, spending more and more time confined to her bed.

The defeat of Germany and her allies in November 1918 had spelled the end for all sovereign heads of state. William II abdicated as German Emperor and King of Prussia on 9 November, and on the following day Bernhard likewise relinquished his title of Duke under pressure from the Meiningen Workers' and Soldiers' Council. His younger half-brother Ernst waived his rights to the succession, such as they were, on 12 November, and the duchy passed into history.

Throughout the years, Charlotte had remained friendly with the Dowager Duchess of Saxe-Coburg Gotha, one of the only true kindred spirits in the family she had ever known. The latter's husband, Duke Alfred, had died in 1900, seventeen months after the suicide of their son and heir. He had thus been spared seeing the outbreak of war between Britain and Germany. His widow, Dowager Duchess Marie, lived long enough to see the collapse of

Tsarist Russia and the brutal killings of so many of her Romanov relations.

Her forgiving eldest daughter Marie, Queen of Roumania, which had been one of the victorious states in 1918, wrote poignantly and sympathetically that Charlotte, 'a shadow of her former self, would still go to Coburg to visit my broken-hearted mother who lived to see the destruction of her kith and kin in Russia'.[1] Yet as Charlotte was spending much of her time virtually bedridden or at least confined to her house, it was an almost impossible effort for her to travel anywhere, and there can have been few if any visits after the end of the war. Moreover, one must assume that she never managed to make it up with her daughter.

To add to Charlotte's other woes she was now suffering from cardiac problems. Early in 1919 she complained of an infection of the colon, and cramp-like digestive pains, which were giving her heart trouble. Too weak to do little more than lie in bed, she found that sleep was often denied her. After a particularly bad night in July she wrote to Schweninger about how she had spent several hours tossing and turning in pain until 4.00 a.m., moving her upper body about, applying compresses and massage, but nothing seemed to help for more than a very short time. The pain was even worse when she tried to walk, though she did her best to try and manage without medicine or morphine.[2]

The widowed Princess Adolf of Schaumburg-Lippe noted how her sister's state of health gave them all cause for anxiety. 'She constantly wrote to me mentioning that she was in great pain, but that I was not to worry about it as she was sure to recover.'[3] But Victoria must have recognised that such optimistic words masked no more than a vain illusion, and been aware that she probably did not have much time left.

In the autumn of 1919 Charlotte left Meiningen for the last time for the clinic at Baden-Baden where she was to undergo further treatment, but now no remedy could do anything for her. On 1 October, two months after her fifty-ninth birthday, with Groddeck at her side, she succumbed to a heart attack. After years of chronic pain and increasing illness, her passing away must have come as a merciful relief.

'My sister's death was quite an unexpected loss,' Margaret wrote in November to her friend Hilda, Lady Corkran, a lady-in-waiting to their aunt Princess Beatrice in England. She had seen very little of Charlotte during the previous few years, and the news therefore came as quite a shock. 'I had no idea how ill she was, &

she evidently thank God did not know it herself, for she was still full of plans, & never alluded to anything in her letters. She must have suffered agonies, & one can but be grateful that she was spared more pain, & that the end came so quickly & peacefully.'4

Bernhard spent his remaining eight years at Schloss Altenstein in Bad Liebenstein. After a short illness he died on 16 January 1928, aged seventy-six. At the time of his death he was the senior surviving colonel-general of the old German imperial army. His coffin lay in state at the palace in Meiningen. Four days later, the population of the city lined the streets in respect as a funeral procession carried it to the station where it was transferred to the train on its last journey to Schloss Altenstein, where he was laid to rest next to Charlotte at a mausoleum in the gardens.

Meanwhile their friend Marie, Dowager Duchess of Saxe-Coburg, had died at Zurich in October 1920, twelve months after Charlotte. Unlike them she had spent her last years in poverty, having lived to see many of her relations in Russia perish at the hands of the Bolsheviks.

By this time a veil had fallen over the life of the unhappy Feodora, and the facts about her remaining days are but few. She disappears almost completely from history. Despite her chronic ill health, between the wars she and her husband were able to pay occasional private visits to England. As they were comparatively minor German royalties of no political significance there would never be any animosity towards them, as there would probably have been towards other, more senior members of her mother's family. Sophie, the former Queen of Greece, occasionally returned briefly to the land of her mother's birth, but neither the former German Emperor nor any of their other siblings ever did so. For their brother Henry and their youngest sister Margaret, both of whom had spent many happy times in England on a regular basis prior to the outbreak of war in August 1914, it was a wrench.

Just twice did *The Times* record the movements of Prince and Princess Henry of Reuss in London during the inter-war years. In June 1932 they were both among a large party of guests present at a reception in Park Street, Grosvenor Square, for the marriage of Captain Henry Broughton. In May 1934 Feodora, apparently without Henry, stayed in London and attended a concert of the Finnish National Orchestra at Queens Hall, and she was also present at a reception at Bryanston Square afterwards.

Henry died on 22 March 1939 at the age of seventy-four, just six months before the outbreak of the Second World War. He was laid to rest in a mausoleum in the woods south of Hirschberg, Silesia. Feodora, his wife and now his widow, had long since been an inmate of the Sanatorium Buchwald-Hohenwiese, less than a mile away. The princess who had so desperately wanted children of her own had instead continued to battle with constant physical ailments, insomnia and severe depression, and endured many years of chronic ill-health similar to that of her mother. A lonely woman with no siblings or close relations in whom to confide, the child of a couple who had perhaps never really wanted children, married for years to a husband who lacked sensitivity and thought she had become a professional self-pitying invalid, her story was a sorry one.

These factors all took their toll, and at length she had nothing to live for. It was said that for her the last straw was when she learnt that south-west Silesia had been ceded to Poland as a result of the Potsdam conference which followed the end of the Second World War and total defeat for Germany.

On 26 August 1945, at the age of sixty-six, she made a suicide pact with her companion Meta Schwenck and put her head in the gas oven. Her body was buried in a vault in the woods near the clinic, where her husband had also been laid to rest. It was a pathetic death which passed virtually unnoticed, and it is ironic that neither she nor her mother, dying not long after the end of both world wars, were ever accorded an obituary in *The Times*. Her mother's death had been mentioned in one sentence in a 'news in brief', while the passing of Bernhard had merited a short paragraph. Feodora, like her husband, passed away unnoticed by the newspaper.

Even after her demise she did not find the peace for which she had craved so long. Her grave was opened and repeatedly vandalised by would-be robbers. Some fifty years later, the historian and biographer Professor John Röhl and his colleagues came to inspect her bones and take samples from them in pursuit of their theory that she had suffered from porphyria. They discovered that several of them were missing. It was a pathetic postscript to a life that had known more than its fair share of frustration, sadness and poor health.

Crown Prince and Princess Frederick William of Prussia

*Crown Princess Frederick William of Prussia with Prince William
and Princess Charlotte, 1861*

*Crown Princess Frederick William of Prussia
with Princess Charlotte, c.1863*

Princess Charlotte, c.1876

Princess Charlotte, Hereditary Princess of Saxe-Meiningen

Prince Bernhard, Hereditary Prince of Saxe-Meiningen

George II, Grand Duke of Saxe-Meiningen from 1866 to 1914

Ellen Franz, the former actress and morganatic third wife of the Grand Duke, later created Baroness von Heldburg, c.1870

Princess Charlotte and Princess Feodora as a baby, 1879

Princess Charlotte and Princess Feodora, 1880

Prince and Princess Bernhard of Saxe-Meiningen

Princess Charlotte of Saxe-Meiningen, 1883

Four generations: Queen Victoria, Crown Princess Frederick William, Princess Charlotte and Princess Feodora, 1884

[OPPOSITE]

Queen Victoria and members of her family at Coburg for the wedding of her grandchildren Ernest, Grand Duke of Hesse and the Rhine and Princess Victoria Melita of Edinburgh, April 1894

Seated, left to right: William II, German Emperor; Queen Victoria; the Empress Frederick; with Princess Beatrice of Saxe-Coburg Gotha and Princess Feodora of Saxe-Meiningen at front

First standing row, left to right: Prince Alfred of Saxe-Coburg Gotha; Nicholas, Tsarevich of Russia; Princess Alix of Hesse and the Rhine; Princess Louis of Battenberg; Princess Henry of Prussia; Grand Duchess Vladimir of Russia; Marie, Duchess of Saxe-Coburg Gotha

Second standing row, left to right: Albert Edward, Prince of Wales; Princess Henry of Battenberg; Princess Philip of Saxe-Coburg Kohary (facing her left); Charlotte, Hereditary Princess of Saxe-Meiningen; Princess Aribert of Anhalt; Louise, Duchess of Connaught

Two standing rows at back, left to right: Prince Louis of Battenberg; Grand Duke Paul of Russia; Prince Henry of Battenberg; Prince Philip of Saxe-Coburg Kohary; Albert, Count Mensdorff; Grand Duke Serge of Russia; Crown Princess and Crown Prince Ferdinand of Roumania; Grand Duchess Serge of Russia; Alfred, Duke of Saxe-Coburg Gotha

Princesses Charlotte and Feodora (both at front) in Roumania with the royal family, with King Carol and Crown Princess Ferdinand between them. Standing behind, Prince William of Hohenzollern-Sigmaringen, his brother Crown Prince Ferdinand, their father Leopold of Hohenzollern-Sigmaringen, brother of King Carol), and Prince Bernhard, c.1896

Princess Feodora and Prince Henry on their wedding day,
September 1898

A postcard commemorating the wedding of
Princess Feodora and Prince Henry

Prince and Princess Henry of Reuss shortly after their marriage

Prince Henry XXX of Reuss

The Empress Frederick (centre) with Princesses Feodora (left) and Charlotte (right) on the terrace at Friedrichshof, c.1898

Princess Feodora, Princess Henry of Reuss

Prince Bernhard (centre) on manoeuvres with King George I and Queen Olga of Greece (both on left) and others, including his nephew Prince Waldemar of Prussia, c.1912

The burial place of and monument to the Hereditary Prince and Princess of Saxe-Meiningen, at Schloss Altenstein, Bad Liebenstein

The family of Princess Charlotte

Parents:

Frederick III, German Emperor and King of Prussia (1831-88, reigned March-June 1888)
Victoria, Princess Royal of Great Britain (1840-1901)

Brothers and sisters:

William II, German Emperor and King of Prussia (1859-1941), m. (1) Augusta Victoria of Schleswig-Holstein (1858-1921), m. (2) Hermine of Reuss (1887-1947)
Henry (1862-1929), m. Irene of Hesse and the Rhine (1866-1953)
Sigismund (1864-66)
Victoria (1866-1929), m. (1) Adolf of Schaumburg-Lippe (1859-1916), m. (2) Alexander Zoubkoff (c.1900-36)
Waldemar (1868-79)
Sophie (1870-1932), m. Constantine, King of Greece (1868-1923)
Margaret (1872-1954), m. Frederick Charles, Landgrave of Hesse-Cassel (1868-1940)

The family of Prince Bernhard

Parents:

George II, Duke of Saxe-Meiningen (1826-1914, reigned 1866-1914)
Charlotte Frederica of Prussia (1831-55) – married 1850

Brothers and sisters:

Georg Albrecht (1852-5)
Marie Elisabeth (1853-1923)
Unnamed son (b. & d.1855, lived only a few hours)

Half-brothers, by stepmother Feodora of Hohenlohe-Langenburg (1839-72) – married 1858:

Ernst Bernhard (1859-1941), m. Katharina Jensen (morganatically)
Frederick John (1861-1914), m. Countess Adelaide of Lippe-Biesterfeld [grandparents of Regina of Saxe-Meiningen, wife of Otto, last Crown Prince of Austria-Hungary]
Victor (b. & d.1865, lived only three days)

George II married a third time in 1873, morganatically, Ellen Franz, created Baroness von Heldburg (1839-1923), no children

Reference Notes

Abbreviations:

BH – Baroness Heldburg
C – Princess Charlotte, later Hereditary Princess and Duchess of Saxe-Meiningen
F – Prince Frederick William, later Crown Prince and Emperor Frederick III
H – Prince Herman of Hohenlohe-Langenburg
S – Dr Schweninger
V – Princess Frederick William, later Crown Princess, Empress Victoria, and Empress Frederick
VASL – Princess Victoria of Prussia, later Princess Adolf of Schaumburg-Lippe
W – Prince William, subsequently Crown Prince and Emperor William II

Chapter 1

1 Röhl, *Wilhelm 1859-1888*, 68-9, V to Prince Albert, 27.1.1860
2 Victoria, Queen, *Dearest Child*, 266, QV to V, 25.7.1860
3 ibid, 267, QV to V, 1.8.1860
4 Röhl, *Wilhelm 1859-1888*, V to Prince Albert, 30.7.1860
5 Victoria, Queen, *Dearest Child*, 268, QV to V, 6.8.1860
6 Pakula, 138, QV to V, 7.8.1860
7 ibid, 138, V, to QV, 10.8.1860
8 Cecil, I, V to QV, 2.11.1860
9 Röhl, *Wilhelm 1859-1888*, 101
10 ibid, 107, V to F, 2.5.1862
11 ibid, 106, V to QV, 23.5.1863
12 ibid, 107, V to F, 9.5.1864
13 Corti, *English Empress*, 114
14 Röhl, *Wilhelm 1859-1888*, 120
15 Victoria, Queen, *Dearest Mama*, 272, 26.9.1863, V to QV, 26.9.1863
16 Victoria, Queen, *Your Dear Letter*, 26, V to QV, 17.5.1865
17 Röhl, *Wilhelm 1859-1888*, 107, V to F, 9.7.1866
18 Victoria, Queen, *Your Dear Letter*, 81, V to QV, 16.7.1866
19 ibid, 107, V to QV, 6.9.1868
20 Longford, 386
21 Croft, 28
22 Röhl, *Wilhelm 1859-1888*, V to F, 21.8.1872

23 Victoria, Queen, *Darling Child*, 138-9, V to QV, 23.5.1874
24 ibid, 163, QV to V, 18.11.1874
25 *Recollections of Three Kaisers,* 73-4

Chapter 2

1 Koller, 53
2 Fontenoy
3 Victoria, Queen, *Darling Child*, 257, V to QV 11.10.1877
4 Röhl, *Wilhelm 1859-1888*, 272, V to QV, 9.9.1877
5 ibid, 107, V to F, 28.10.1877
6 Pakula, 371, V to QV, 21.7.1877
7 ibid, 371, QV to V, 25.7.1877
8 Victoria, Queen, *Darling Child*, 261, V to QV, 23.8.1877
9 ibid, 282, V to QV, 19.2.1878
10 Lee I, 432
11 Alice, 359, 363
12 *The Times*, 19.2.1878
13 as 12
14 Victoria, Queen, *Darling Child,* 282, V to QV, 19.2.1878
15 Croft, 301
16 *The Times*, 19.2.1878
17 Victoria, *My memoirs*, 47
18 Radziwill, 144
19 Pakula, 372, V to QV, 19.2.1878

Chapter 3

1 William II, 147
2 Bennett, 212
3 Roberts, 182
4 Röhl, *Wilhelm 1859-1888*, 107, V to QV, 9.9.1879
5 ibid, 370, V to F, 10.9.1879
6 ibid, 379, C to V, 1.10.1879
7 ibid, 379, C to V, 24.11.1879
8 ibid, 379, C to V, 14.12.1879
9 ibid, 379, C to V, 18.12.1879
10 ibid, 380, C to V, 21.12.1879
11 ibid, 365, V to F, 7.12.1879
12 ibid, 354, C to V, 13.5.1880
13 ibid, 359, 12.5.1880, F to V
14 ibid, 355, F to V, 23.8.1880
15 Bennett, 214
16 Victoria, Queen, *Beloved Mama*, 67, QV to V, 5.3.1880

17 ibid, 108, QV to V, 25.10.1881
18 ibid, 85, QV to V, 31.7.1880
19 Fontenoy
18 Röhl, *Wilhelm 1859-1888*, 383, C to V, 3.8.1881
19 ibid, 383, C to H, 17.12.1881
20 ibid, 383, C to H, 2.1.1882
21 ibid, 383, C to H, 15.3.1882
22 ibid, 523, C to V, 9.1.1885
23 ibid, 109, V to Duchess of Connaught, 2.1.1885
24 Victoria, Queen, *Beloved and Darling Child* 53, QV to V, 5.7.1887
25 Pakula 513, V to QV, 2.11.1888

Chapter 4

1 Röhl, *Wilhelm 1888-1900*, 10; *Letters EF*, 322-3, V to QV, 29.6.1888
2 Röhl, *Wilhelm 1859-1888*, 107-8, V, diary, 24.7.1888
3 Röhl, *Wilhelm 1888-1900*, 55, V to QV, 26.9.1888
4 Marie I, 222-3
5 ibid, 224
6 Röhl, *Wilhelm 1888-1900*, 641-2, Empress Augusta Victoria to W, 21.7.1890
7 as 6
8 Röhl, Warren & Hunt, 156
9 as 8
10 Röhl, *Wilhelm 1888-1900*, 633, EF to VASL, 5.12.1890
11 ibid, 633, EF to Baroness Stockmar, 5.4.1891
12 ibid, 633, EF to VASL, 4.6.1891
13 ibid, 635, EF to VASL, 24.2.1891
14 ibid, 636, V to QV, 31.3.1891
15 ibid, 635, EF to VASL, 15.11.1891
16 ibid, 635, EF to VASL, 8.1.1893
17 Fischer, 311
18 Röhl, *Wilhelm 1888-1900*, 627
19 ibid, 660, Ernest of Hohenlohe-Langenburg to George, Duke of Saxe-Meiningen, 10.1.1892
20 Victoria, *Empress Frederick writes to Sophie*, 89

Chapter 5

1 Fischer, 221
2 Röhl, *Wilhelm 1888-1900*, 636-7, C to BH, 25.3.1895
3 Fontenoy
4 Röhl, *Wilhelm 1888-1900*, 637, Waldersee diary, 24.3.1895
5 Fischer 347

6 Fontenoy

7 Victoria, *Empress Frederick writes to Sophie*, 143

8 Röhl, *Wilhelm 1888-1900*, 670, C to BH, 14.4.1895

9 ibid, 675, C to BH, 26.6.1894

10 ibid, 675, C to BH, 20.5.1895

11 ibid, 637, C to BH, 14.6.1895

12 ibid, 635, C to BH, 7.9.1896

13 ibid, 638-9

14 Fontenoy

15 Victoria, *Empress Frederick writes to Sophie*, 151

16 Marie I, 264-5

17 as 15

18 Pakula, 561, V to QV, 30.9.1893

19 ibid, V to QV, 5.10.1894

20 Röhl, Warren & Hunt, 157

21 Mandache, 292, Duchess of Saxe-Coburg to Crown Princess of Roumania, 5.5.1897

22 Victoria of Prussia, *My memoirs*, 79

23 Victoria, *Empress Frederick writes to Sophie*, 261

24 Mandache, 317-8, Duchess of Saxe-Coburg to Crown Princess of Roumania, 3.10.1897

Chapter 6

1 Fontenoy

2 Victoria, *Empress Frederick writes to Sophie*, 284

3 *Freeman's Journal and Daily Commercial Advertiser*, 21.10.1898

4 Fischer, 341

5 *North-Eastern Daily Gazette*, 17.2.1899

6 Mandache 438, Duchess of Saxe-Coburg to Crown Princess of Roumania, 16.7.1900

7 Röhl, Warren & Hunt, 158

8 Cecil, II, 63

9 Noel, 80

10 Croft, 300

11 Röhl, Warren & Hunt, 158

12 ibid, Prince Bernhard of Saxe-Meiningen to BH, 8.4.1900

13 ibid, 158, C to BH, 9.8.1900

14 Victoria, *Empress Frederick writes to Sophie*, 332

15 Mandache 451, Duchess of Saxe-Coburg to Crown Princess of Roumania, 31.10.1900

16 Victoria, *Empress Frederick writes to Sophie*, 336

17 Röhl, III, 79, C to S, undated

18 Röhl, Warren & Hunt, 159, C to BH, 5.12.1900

19 ibid, 159, C to BH, 28.3.1901

Chapter 7

1 Victoria of Prussia, *My memoirs,* 162
2 ibid, 109
3 Röhl, *Wilhelm 1859-1888,* 109, C to S and Lena S, 26.6.03
4 ibid, 109-10, C to S, 1.4.1906
5 Croft, 301
6 Röhl, *Wilhelm 1859-1888,* 110, C to S, 23.11.1906
7 ibid, 110, C to S, 3.12.1906
8 ibid, 110, C to S, 24.12.1906
9 ibid, 110, C to S, 25.4.1907
10 ibid, 110, C to S, 18.11.1907
11 Röhl, Warren & Hunt, 162, F to BH, 2.8.1905
12 ibid, 162, C to BH, 15.5.1905
13 ibid, 163, F to BH, 6.7.1909
14 ibid, 166, F to BH, 23.3.1910
15 ibid, 168-9, C to F, 14.9.1911
16 ibid, 170, C to BH, 29.5.1912
17 Röhl, *Wilhelm 1900-1941*, 148, C to S, 4.4.1901
18 ibid, 158, C to S, 26.6.1903
19 ibid, 158, C to S, 24.12.1906
20 ibid, 556, C to S, 10.11.1907
21 ibid, 556, C to S, 18.11.1907
22 ibid, 566, C to S, 24.2.1907
23 Röhl, *Wilhelm 1888-1900*, 675, C to S, 5.12.1908
24 ibid, 111, C to S, 14.1.1909
25 ibid, 111, C to S, 16.1.1909
26 ibid, 112, C to S, 5.11.1909
27 Röhl, Warren & Hunt, 153, C to BH, 25.7.11
28 Van der Kiste, *Prince Henry*, 92
29 Röhl, Warren & Hunt, 153, F to BH, 18.7.1911
30 Röhl, *Wilhelm 1900-1941*, 1131, 18.7.12, C to S
31 Röhl, *Wilhelm 1888-1900*, 898, C to S, 25.11.1912

Chapter 8

1 *New York Times,* 19.7.1914
2 Röhl, Warren & Hunt, 154, C to S, 12.1.1918
3 ibid, 177, Henry of Reuss to BH, 3.2.1916
4 as 3
5 ibid, 178, Henry of Reuss to BH, 2.3.1916
6 ibid, 179, Henry of Reuss to BH, 25.6.1916

7 ibid, 179
8 Victoria of Prussia, *My memoirs*, 109

Chapter 9

1 Marie of Roumania, I, 226
2 Röhl, Warren & Hunt, 154, 6.7.1919
3 Victoria of Prussia, *My memoirs*, 199
4 Van der Kiste, *Prussian Princesses*, 96-7, Princess Margaret to Lady Corkran, 17.11.1919

Bibliography

Books

The place of publication in London unless otherwise stated

Alice, Grand Duchess of Hesse, *Biographical sketch and letters,* John Murray, 1884

Anon., *Recollections of three Kaisers,* Herbert Jenkins, 1929

Barkeley, Richard, *The Empress Frederick, Daughter of Queen Victoria,* Macmillan, 1956

Bennett, Daphne, *Vicky, Princess Royal of England and German Empress,* Collins Harvill, 1971

Cecil, Lamar, *Wilhelm II: Prince and Emperor, 1859-1900,* Chapel Hill, University of North Carolina, 1989

-- *Wilhelm II: Emperor and Exile, 1900-1941,* Chapel Hill, University of North Carolina, 1996

Corti, Egon Caesar Conte, *The English Empress: A study in the relations between Queen Victoria and her eldest daughter, Empress Frederick of Germany,* Cassell, 1957

Croft, Christina, *Queen Victoria's granddaughters, 1860-1918,* Hilliard & Croft, 2013

Epton, Nina, *Victoria and her daughters,* Weidenfeld & Nicolson, 1971

Fischer, Henry W., *The Private Lives of William II & his Consort: A Secret History of the Court of Berlin*, Heinemann, 1904

Fontenoy, Mme La Marquise de [Margaret Cunliffe-Owen], *The Secret Memoirs of the Courts of Europe: William II, Germany; Francis Joseph, Austria-Hungary*, Vol 1 (of 2), Philadelphia: Barrie, 1900; online http://www.gutenberg.org/ebooks/12548, accessed April 2015

Gelardi, Julia P., *Born to rule: Granddaughters of Victoria, Queens of Europe,* Headline, 2004

Koller, Ann Marie, *The Theater Duke: George II of Saxe-Meiningen and the German Stage,* Stanford University Press, 1984

Lee, Sir Sidney, *King Edward VII, Vol. I: From birth to accession,* Macmillan, 1925

Longford, Elizabeth, *Victoria R.I.,* Weidenfeld & Nicolson, 1964

Magnus, Philip, *King Edward the Seventh,* John Murray, 1964

Marie, Duchess of Edinburgh, *Dearest Missy: The correspondence between Marie, Grand Duchess of Russia, Duchess of Edinburgh and of Saxe-Coburg and Gotha and her daughter, Marie, Crown Princess of Roumania, 1879-1900,* ed. Diana Mandache, Falkoping, Sweden, Rosvall Royal Books, 2011

Marie, Queen of Roumania, *The story of my life,* 3 vols, Cassell, 1934-5

Noel, Gerard, *Princess Alice, Queen Victoria's Forgotten Daughter,* Constable, 1974

Pakula, Hannah, *An uncommon woman: The Empress Frederick,* Weidenfeld & Nicolson, 1996

Radziwill, Princess Catherine, *The Empress Frederick,* Cassell, 1934

Roberts, Dorothea, *Two royal lives: Gleanings from Berlin and from the lives of Their Imperial Highnesses the Crown Prince and Princess of Germany,* T. Fisher Unwin, 1887

Röhl, John, *The Kaiser and his Court: Wilhelm II and the Government of Germany,* Cambridge University Press, 1996

-- *Wilhelm II: The Kaiser's personal monarchy, 1888-1900,* Cambridge University Press, 2004

-- *Wilhelm II: Into the abyss of war and exile, 1900-1941,* Cambridge University Press, 2014

-- *Young Wilhelm: The Kaiser's early life, 1859-1888,* Cambridge University Press, 1998

Röhl, John, Warren, Martin, & Hunt, David, *Purple Secret: Genes, 'Madness', and the Royal Houses of Europe,* Bantam, 1998

Sinclair, Andrew, *The other Victoria: The Princess Royal and the great game of Europe,* Weidenfeld & Nicolson, 1981

Van der Kiste, John, *Dearest Vicky, Darling Fritz: Queen Victoria's Eldest Daughter and the German Emperor,* Stroud, Sutton, 2001

-- *Kaiser Wilhelm II: Germany's last Emperor,* Stroud, Sutton, 1999

-- *Prince Henry of Prussia, 1862-1929,* South Brent, A & F/CreateSpace, 2015

-- *The Prussian Princesses: Sisters of Kaiser Wilhelm II,* Stroud, Fonthill Media, 2014

Vovk, Justin C., *Imperial requiem: Four royal women and the fall of the age of empires,* Bloomington, iUniverse, 2012

-- *Kaiser Wilhelm II: Germany's Last Emperor,* Sutton, 1999

Victoria, Consort of Frederick III, German Emperor, *The Empress Frederick writes to Sophie,* ed. Arthur Gould Lee, Faber, 1955

-- *Letters of the Empress Frederick,* ed. Sir Frederick Ponsonby, Macmillan, 1928

Victoria, Queen, *The Letters of Queen Victoria: a Selection from Her Majesty's Correspondence between the years 1837 and 1861,* ed. A.C. Benson & Viscount Esher, 3 vols, John Murray, 1907

-- *The Letters of Queen Victoria, 2nd Series: a Selection from Her Majesty's Correspondence and Journal between the years 1862 and 1885,* ed. G. E. Buckle, 3 vols, John Murray, 1926-8

-- *The Letters of Queen Victoria, 3rd Series: a Selection from Her Majesty's Correspondence and Journal between the years 1886 and 1901,* ed. G.E. Buckle, 3 vols, John Murray, 1930-2

-- *Dearest Child: Letters between Queen Victoria and the Princess Royal, 1858-1861;* ed. Roger Fulford, Evans Bros, 1964

-- *Dearest Mama: Private Correspondence of Queen Victoria and the Crown Princess of Prussia, 1861-1864;* ed. Roger Fulford, Evans Bros, 1968

-- *Your Dear Letter: Private Correspondence of Queen Victoria and the Crown Princess of Prussia, 1865-1871,* ed. Roger Fulford, Evans Bros, 1971

-- *Darling Child: Private Correspondence of Queen Victoria and the Crown Princess of Prussia, 1871-1878;* ed. Roger Fulford, Evans Bros, 1976

-- *Beloved Mama: Private Correspondence of Queen Victoria and the German Crown Princess of Prussia, 1878-1885;* ed. Roger Fulford, Evans Bros, 1981

Victoria of Prussia, Princess, *My Memoirs*, Eveleigh, Nash & Grayson, 1929; Royalty Digest, 1996

Vickers, Hugo, *Alice, Princess Andrew of Greece*, Viking, 2000

Weintraub, Stanley, *Victoria: Biography of a Queen,* Unwin Hyman, 1987

William II, *My early life,* Methuen, 1926

Zeepvat, Charlotte, *Queen Victoria's family: A century of photographs 1840-1940,* Stroud: Sutton, 2001

Journal articles

Lalor, William Mead, 'Charlotte of Prussia – the elegant cousin Charly'. *Royalty Digest*, Vol V, No 9, March 1996

Van der Kiste, John, 'Charley the Pretender': Charlotte of Prussia, Hereditary Princess of Saxe-Meiningen. *European Royal History Journal*, XVIII, Jul/Aug 2000

-- 'A strange little creature: Princess Feodora of Saxe-Meiningen'. *Royalty Digest*, Vol VIII, No 6, December 1998

Zeepvat, Charlotte, 'Kirche, Küche, Kinder...or perhaps not'. *Royalty Digest*, Vol. VIII, March and April 1999 (two parts)

Newspapers

European Royal History Journal
Freeman's Journal and Daily Commercial Advertiser
The Guardian
New York Times
North-Eastern Daily Gazette
Pall Mall Gazette
Royalty Digest
The Times

Index

B – Bernhard, Duke of Saxe-Meiningen
C- Charlotte
F – Feodora

public life, 50; at Cannes, 60; and differences with F, 61, 64; and axe attack on carriage, 66; and F's alleged 'fearful lies' to get money from her grandmother, 69; silver wedding, 70; forcible retirement from army, 79; succeeds his father as Duke of Saxe-Meiningen, 81; and First World War, 82; relinquishes title of Grand Duke, 87; death, 89

Charlotte of Prussia, Princess, later Princess of Saxe-Meiningen (1831-55), 14

Charlotte of Prussia, Princess, later Empress Alexandra of Russia (1798-1860), 6

Charlotte of the Belgians, Princess, later Carlota, Empress of Mexico (1840-1927), 62

Charlotte of Wales, Princess (1796-1817), 62

Christian Victor of Schleswig-Holstein, Prince (1867-1900), 68

Chronegk, Ludwig, 15

Constantine I, King of Greece (1868-1923), 36, 82

Corkran, Hilda, Lady, formerly Hilda Chichester (1875-1961), 88

Darcourt, Octavie, 25

Diersburg, Karl-Augustus Freiherr Roeder von, 50

Döderlein, Albert, 73, 83

Edward VII, King of England (1841-1910), 7, 11, 18, 45, 66

Edward, Duke of Kent (1767-1820), 62

Elizabeth, Grand Duchess of Oldenburg (18267-96), 19

Elizabeth Anna of Prussia, Princess (1857-95), 18

Elizabeth of Austria, Archduchess (1883-1965), 37

Elizabeth, Queen of Prussia (1801-73), 6

Elizabeth, Queen of Roumania (1843-1916), 35, 52

Elizabeth, Grand Duchess of Oldenburg (1826-96), 19

Ernest, Duke of Saxe-Coburg Gotha (1818-93), 34, 39, 54

Ernest, Grand Duke of Hesse and the Rhine (1868-1937), 54

Ernest Gunther, Duke of Schleswig-Holstein (1863-1921), 48

Ernest, Prince of Saxe-Meiningen (1859-1941), 27, 40

Eulenburg-Hertefeld, Philipp, Prince of (1847-1921), 75-6

Feodora of Hohenlohe-Langenburg, Princess (1839-72), 14

Feodora of Leiningen, Princess, later of Hohenlohe-Langenburg (1807-72), 14

Feodora of Saxe-Meiningen, Princess (1879-1945), birth, 24; Crown Princess's affection for, 28, 37-8, 59; at Queen Victoria's Golden Jubilee, 31; ill-health, 38, 63-4, 73-4, 83-4; slow physical development, 38, 53; and relations with Empress Frederick, 37-8, 54, 59; playmate of Ursula von Kotze, 45; proposals for marriage of, 54; engagement, 54-5; wedding, 57; interests, 59; frustrated hopes of motherhood, 60, 72; and Queen Victoria, 61, 67-8; and differences with C and B, 61, 63-4, 66-7, 69-70; and porphyria, 63; Henry and Irene's sympathy for, 68; 'alleged lies' about financial dependence on grandmother, and accused of having venereal disease, 69; visits to England, 79-80, 89; last years and suicide, 90

Ferdinand, King of Roumania (1865-1927), 35, 51-3

Francis Ferdinand, Archduke of Austria-Hungary (1863-1914), 82

Frank, Dr, 72

Franz, Reinhold, 73

Frederick Augustus II, Grand Duke of Oldenburg (1852-1931), 18

Frederick Charles of Prussia, Prince (1828-85), 18

Frederick Charles, Landgrave of Hesse-Cassel (1868-1940), 43

Frederick III, Emperor, formerly Frederick William, Crown Prince of Prussia and Germany (1831-88), 5, 7, 11, 18, 19, 25-6, 28, 30, 39; and C's attitude towards Augusta Victoria, 27; illness and attendance at Queen Victoria's Golden Jubilee, 31-2; accession and death, 33

Frederick Leopold of Prussia, Prince (1865-1931), 40

Frederick William III, King (1770-1840), 23

Frederick William IV, King of Prussia (1795-1861), 7

George II, Duke of Saxe-Meiningen (1826-1914), 14-5, 81

George III, King (1738-1820), 62

George IV, King (1762-1830), 62

George of Saxe-Meiningen, Prince (1852-5), 14

George V, King of England (1865-1936), 51, 78

Groddeck, George, 71, 87-8

Haedke, Dr, 82

Harden, Maximilian (1861-1927), 75-6

Heim, Dr von, 58

Heldburg, Baroness von, formerly Ellen Franz (1839-1923), 14, 45, 48, 50, 61, 64, 67, 69, 72, 78, 83, 84

Henry of Prussia, Prince (1862-1929), 8, 34, 38, 59, 89; birth, 7; and relationship with C, 33, 40, 67-8, 78; and C and B's silver wedding, 70; F's relationship with, 72

Henry XXX of Reuss, Prince (1864-1939), 59, 61, 67, 68, 70, 72; engagement, 54; wedding, 57; and problems with parents-in-law, 63; and F's ill-health, 82-4; death, 90

Herman, Prince of Hohenlohe-Langenburg (1832-1913), 30

Hinzpeter, Georg (1827-1907), 25

Hochberg, Conrad von, 79

Hohenau, Count Frederick of (1857-1914), 44

Humbert I, King of Italy (1842-1900), 47, 66

Irene of Hesse, Princess, later Princess Henry of Prussia (1866-1953), 55, 57, 68, 70, 72, 78

Karolyi, Countess, 20

Ketteler, Clemens von (1853-1900), 66

Kotze, Elizabeth von (1860-1922), 45, 48-9

Kotze, Leberecht von (1850-1920), 44-5, 48-9

Kotze, Ursula von (1883-1971), 45

Kraepelin, Emil, 54

ALSO BY JOHN VAN DER KISTE

Royal and historical biography

Frederick III (1981)
Queen Victoria's Family: A Select Bibliography (1982)
Dearest Affie [with Bee Jordaan] (1984)
  - revised edition, *Alfred* (2013)
Queen Victoria's Children (1986)
Windsor and Habsburg (1987)
Edward VII's Children (1989)
Princess Victoria Melita (1991)
George V's Children (1991)
George III's Children (1992)
Crowns in a Changing World (1993)
Kings of the Hellenes (1994)
Childhood at Court 1819-1914 (1995)
Northern Crowns (1996)
King George II and Queen Caroline (1997)
The Romanovs 1818-1959 (1998)
Kaiser Wilhelm II (1999)
The Georgian Princesses (2000)
Dearest Vicky, Darling Fritz (2001)
Royal Visits to Devon & Cornwall (2002)
Once a Grand Duchess [with Coryne Hall] (2002)
William and Mary (2003)
Emperor Francis Joseph (2005)
Sons, Servants & Statesmen (2006)
A Divided Kingdom (2007)
William John Wills (2011)
The Prussian Princesses (2014)
The Big Royal Quiz Book (2014)
Prince Henry of Prussia (2015)
The last German Empress (2015)
Princess Helena (2015)

Local history and true crime

Devon Murders (2006)
Devonshire's Own (2007)
Cornish Murders [with Nicola Sly] (2007)
A Grim Almanac of Devon (2008)
Somerset Murders [with Nicola Sly] (2008)
Cornwall's Own (2008)
Plymouth, History and Guide (2009)
A Grim Almanac of Cornwall (2009)
West Country Murders [with Nicola Sly] (2009)
Jonathan Wild (2009)
Durham Murders & Misdemeanours (2009)
Surrey Murders (2009)
Berkshire Murders (2010)
More Cornish Murders [with Nicola Sly] (2010)
Ivybridge & South Brent Through Time [with Kim Van der Kiste]
    (2010)
Dartmoor from old photographs (2010)
A Grim Almanac of Hampshire (2011)
The Little Book of Devon (2011)
More Devon Murders (2011)
More Somerset Murders [with Nicola Sly] (2011)
The Plymouth Book of Days (2011)
The Little Book of Cornwall (2013)
Plymouth, a City at War 1914-45 (2014)

Music

Roxeventies (1982)
Singles File (1987)
Beyond the Summertime [with Derek Wadeson] (1990)
Gilbert & Sullivan's Christmas (2000)
Roy Wood (2014)
The Little Book of The Beatles (2014)
Jeff Lynne (2015)

Fiction

The Man on the Moor (2004)
Olga and David (2014)
Elmore Sounds (2015)

Plays

The Man on the Moor (2015)
A Mere Passing Shadow (2015)

For availability of the above titles, please refer to Amazon.co.uk/ Amazon.com

Printed in Great Britain
by Amazon